# JANUA LINGUARUM

## STUDIA MEMORIAE
## NICOLAI VAN WIJK DEDICATA

*edenda curat*

C. H. VAN SCHOONEVELD

*Indiana University*

*Series Minor, 148*

# THE SPEECH OF PRIMATES

*by*

## PHILIP LIEBERMAN

*University of Connecticut*
*Haskins Laboratories*

1972

MOUTON

THE HAGUE · PARIS

Printed in The Netherlands by Dijkstra Niemeyer printers, Groningen

# ACKNOWLEDGMENTS

Permission to reprint the following articles is gratefully acknowledged:

"Newborn Infant Cry and Nonhuman Primate Vocalizations", co-authors: Katharine S. Harris, Peter Wolff, and Lorraine H. Russell, from *Journal of Speech and Hearing Research* 14 (1971), 718-727.

"On the Acoustic Analysis of Primate Vocalizations", from *Behavior Research Methods & Instrumentation* 1 (1969), 169-174.

"On the Speech of Neanderthal Man", co-author: Edmund S. Crelin, from *Linguistic Inquiry* 2 (1971), 203-222. © 1971 by the Massachusetts Institute of Technology.

"Phonetic Ability and Related Anatomy of the Newborn and Adult Human, Neanderthal Man and the Chimpanzee", co-authors: Edmund S. Crelin and Dennis H. Klatt, from *American Anthropologist* 74:2 (1972).

"Primate Vocalizations and Human Linguistic Ability", from *The Journal of the Acoustical Society of America* 44 (1968), 1574-1584. © 1969 by the Acoustical Society of America.

"Vocal Tract Limitations on the Vocal Repertoires of Rhesus Monkey and Other Non-Human Primates", co-authors: Dennis H. Klatt and William A. Wilson, from *Science* 164 (1969), 1185-1187. © 1969 by the American Association for the Advancement of Science.

# TABLE OF CONTENTS

# INTRODUCTION

This collection of papers has been deliberately entitled *The Speech of Primates* rather than *Vocalizations* or *Acoustic Signals of Primates*, because of the significance of the term 'speech'. In linguistic usage, speech implies the presence of language. Linguists have generally made the unsupported assertion that only human beings possess language; language is supposed to be a uniquely human behavioral attribute, and the communication systems of all other animals are supposed to be non-linguistic. According to this viewpoint, language is a phenomenon that has no 'non-trivial' parallels or antecedents in the communications of other animals. Human language is thus assumed to be the result of a special act of creation or the result of some 'unique' and 'abrupt' evolutionary event.[1] The studies that form the body of this volume refute this unfortunately common view concerning the 'unique' basis of human language.

These studies show that the supralaryngeal vocal tract of modern man has gradually evolved for the purpose of enhancing rapid communication by means of speech. Although language is clearly possible in the absence of human speech, it is less rapid and efficient. Human language depends crucially on the ability of all human beings to produce and to perceive the sounds of human speech. These sounds have a special role in human language; they make rapid communication possible.

The rate at which *homo sapiens* transmits information by speech

---

[1]  It is difficult to state when this tradition started. It is manifested in the works of Descartes, and carries through into recent studies like that of Lenneburg (1967).

is almost ten times faster than the rate that can be achieved through any other single sensory channel. 'Simple' auditory non-speech signals, such as clicks, fuse into unresolvable 'buzzes' at rates of 20 to 30 clicks per second. The phonetic elements of speech, the individual segments, (e.g. the sounds [b], [a] and [t] of the word *bat*) are resolved and identified at these same rates during normal speech. The rate of information transfer of human speech, for purposes of comparison, exceeds the fusion frequency of the human visual system. (Motion pictures are possible because the human visual system fuses images when they are presented at a rate of 16 pictures per second.)

The rapid rate of human speech is achieved by means of a process of 'encoding' in which the acoustic cues that signal various sequences of consonants and vowels are collapsed into syllable-sized segments. The unitary, syllable-sized sound bundles are transmitted at a slower rate of about 7 segments per second, which is within the perceptual limits set by the temporal resolving power of the human auditory system. Human listeners restore the high data rate by 'decoding' the acoustic syllable-sized bundles in terms of the consonant and vowel sequences that make up the individual syllables. This 'decoding' involves restructuring the acoustic signal in terms of the articulatory gestures and the speech producing apparatus that produced a particular speech signal. We will discuss in the following papers the special acoustic properties of sounds like the human vowels /a/, /i/ and /u/ that make this process possible. These sounds can only be produced with a human-like supralaryngeal vocal tract. The mutations that have been retained in *homo sapiens* which make human speech possible result in reduced respiratory efficiency, less efficient chewing, and a greater propensity to choke on food compared to non-human primates or to earlier, extinct hominids, e.g. classic Neanderthal man. These now extinct hominids lacked 'articulate' human speech. They were otherwise better adapted for the vegetative functions of life.

Human speech therefore is one of the central aspects of human language. Rather than being an arbitrary and fortuitously determined level of language it is an essential defining characteristic of human language. The sounds of human speech are the *only* sounds that will suffice for human language. This does not mean that a communication system that is equivalent functionally to human language could not evolve, using some other means of 'phonetic' signalling. Primates have, however, taken this particular path towards speech.[2] We can thus make valid inferences on the evolution of human language by studying the evolution of the human vocal apparatus.

Modern man's speech-producing mechanism has clearly evolved, through the Darwinian process of mutation and natural selection, from an ancestral form that is similar to the vocal apparatus of living non-human primates. Living non-human primates lack the anatomic apparatus that is necessary to produce the full range of sounds of human speech. Monkeys and apes inherently could not produce 'articulate' human speech even if they had the requisite mental ability. These animals, however, retain the phonetic basis for a language. Some of the phonetic features that play a part in human language can be seen in the communications of living non-human primates. All non-human primates as well as many other animals, for example, appear to differentiate their speech signals by modulating the fundamental frequency of phonation. This is hardly surprising since these animals have larynges that are similar to the human larynx. As Negus (1949) pointed out, these larynges have evolved modifications that enhance phonetic ability at the expense of respiratory efficiency. The modulations of fundamental frequency that play a part in the communications of non-human primates[3]

---

[2] Completely different methods could be developed to evolve the phonetic basis of a non-human language. Birds, for example, have a rather different sound-producing system (Greenewalt, 1967). There is no reason to expect the communications of birds to be structured in terms of the same acoustic factors as primates. A complex bird language could evolve, in principle, that would be quite different from human language. The situation is perhaps analogous to the evolution of the anatomical prerequisites for tool using. Primates freed their hands for the use of tools by developing erect posture. Sea otters, however, *Enhydra lutris* (Kenyon, 1969) make use of tools (large rocks which they use to open mollusk crustaceans) by floating on their backs to free their flippers.

[3] The communications of more common animals like dogs, cats, or wolves also have not been systematically investigated. In fact, despite various dogmatic assertions comparing human and animal communication, we really do not know how any species of animal communicates.

have never been systematically investigated. We really do not know what these animals can communicate by means of acoustic signals. The fact that they have larynges that are specialized for modulating fundamental frequency is suggestive of adaptation for communication.

Recent electrophysiological data (Wollberg and Newman, 1972) demonstrates that non-human primates have neural mechanisms that are structured in terms of some of their meaningful acoustic signals. This is relevant since human phonetic ability appears to involve a match between the constraints imposed by the speech-producing apparatus, which produces certain types of acoustic signals, and the human neural speech-perceiving mechanism (Lieberman, 1970). These same phonetic organizing principles appear to be present in non-human primates as well as simpler animals like frogs (Capranica, 1965). Insights into the structure of the phonetic component of human language undoubtedly will follow from further study of primate communication. Recent experiments involving communication with chimpanzees by sign language (Gardner and Gardner, 1969) and plastic symbols (Premack, 1972) indicate that these animals have many of the 'logical' abilities that the term 'language' implies. The discovery of these animals' natural communication systems would be of signal importance.

Non-human primates may well rely on gestural communications to supplement the limited repertoire of phonetic contrasts at their disposal. Human language may have evolved from the same gestural base. Hewes (1971) presents a convincing argument for the gestural beginnings of language. The most recent reconstructions of the speech-producing anatomy of various fossil hominids by my colleague Edmund S. Crelin indicate that species like *Australopithecus Pleisianthropus* had essentially the same vocal apparatus as present day non-human primates. The phonetic level of early hominid communication may well have been gestural. The development of, or rather the transfer to, vocal communication could have been a consequence of the development of hunting by early hominids. Communication at distance is more readily achieved by means of acoustic signalling. Speech also frees the hands for the unrestricted use of implements and weapons. Mutations that enhanced the range of phonetic possibilities would have been retained because they result-ed in a richer signalling system.

The process of anatomical specialization for human speech dem-onstrates what Sir Arthur Keith termed the "antiquity of man". Our most recent reconstructions and modellings of the speech-pro-ducing anatomy of fossil hominids (Crelin *et al.*, forthcoming) show that hominids like the Steinheim and Skhul V fossils had human-like supralaryngeal vocal tracts. These hominids coexisted (200,000-40,000 years ago) with hominids like classic Neanderthal man, who lacked the supralaryngeal vocal apparatus that is neces-sary for human speech. Although hominids like the Steinheim fos-sil had human-like supralaryngeal vocal tracts 200,000 years ago, they may not have had the neural equipment that is also necessary for the utilization of encoded speech. Differences in phonetic ability, whatever their functional values may have initially been, would have played an important part in the divergence of different breeding populations. There would still, however, be functional reasons for the retention of a supralaryngeal vocal tract that produced the range of human speech even if the speech were at first unencoded. Sounds like the human vowels /a/, /i/ and /u/ are acoustically stable signals (cf. Stevens, 1969 and Lieberman and Crelin, 1971). A hu-man speaker can be imprecise in positioning his tongue when he produces these sounds and still produce acoustic signals that are close to the acoustic signals that would result from the 'ideal' ar-ticulatory maneuver. Other speech sounds like the 'central' vowels /I/, /U/, /ae/, etc., are not as acoustically stable. Small errors in ar-ticulation have relatively great acoustic consequences. Mutations that gradually developed a human-like supralaryngeal vocal tract therefore would be retained since they would enhance vocal com-munication. The process would be gradual, starting on the base represented by fossil hominids that resembled non-human primates. Hominid forms like Rhodesian man appear to represent inter-mediate stages in this evolutionary process since they have supra-laryngeal vocal tracts that are intermediate between *homo sapiens* and non-human primates (Crelin *et al.*, forthcoming).

The total picture that emerges is one in which the anatomical structures that are necessary for human speech production and the neural mechanisms that are also necessary for human speech perception developed either coevally or sequentially. A process of positive feedback may have played a role in this evolutionary process. Vocal tract anatomy that is useful for the production of acoustic signals facilitating speech encoding, would have enhanced the retention of mutations that yielded the necessary neural abilities. It is virtually impossible to determine which came first, the anatomy or the neural ability. If one had to make a guess, the anatomy might be thought to have developed first since the acoustic signals that the human supralaryngeal vocal tract alone can make (with respect to other primates) are more acoustically stable, and hence have an immediate phonetic value. The important point is that the evolutionary process that could account for these changes is, as Charles Darwin (1871) claimed, in principle no different from the evolutionary processes that relate other aspects of human anatomy and physiology to other animals.

The papers that follow should be regarded as starting points for the study of three aspects of human linguistic ability.

First, that adult *homo-sapiens* has a species-specific vocal tract that is necessary for producing the sounds of human speech. The sounds of human speech are necessary for human language. They are not arbitrary; they make rapid acoustic communication possible.

Second, that enhanced linguistic ability was the conditioning factor in the process of natural selection that led to the evolution of the human vocal tract. In other words, that the human vocal tract evolved for the function of speech. The human vocal tract is inferior to the non-human vocal tract with respect to the vegetative functions of breathing, swallowing, and chewing (Lieberman *et al.*, 1972; Manly and Braley, 1950; Manly and Shiere, 1950; Manly and Vinton, 1951). The only function for which the human vocal tract, i.e., the oral cavity, pharynx, larynx, and nose is superior, is generating the full range of sounds of human speech. The morphology of the base of the skull of *homo sapiens* reflects the process of mutation and natural selection that resulted in the development of human speech. Human speech is as important a factor in the late stages of human evolution as chewing and upright posture are in its early stages.

Third, that the evolution of human speech is explicable in terms of the Darwinian process of mutation and natural selection. The process was gradual and human speech is linked to the speech of other animals.

A final note on the papers that make up this collection is perhaps in order. These papers span a five year period and since they were independent studies directed to different audiences, there is a certain degree of redundancy with regard to background information on acoustics. Readers who are not familiar with the articulatory and acoustic aspects of speech production perhaps should first refer to the appropriate sections of papers 4 and 6. The reader can note the formulation of the basic theory that unifies all of these papers in the initial study, "Primate Vocalizations and Human Linguistic Ability". This study, through the technique of acoustic analysis guided by anatomical considerations, demonstrated that living non-human primates lacked the anatomical mechanism that is necessary for the production of human speech. It thus showed that the human vocal apparatus is species-specific. Once this fact was established, it was reasonable to formulate the question of how and when the human vocal apparatus evolved. This was especially pertinent since it was apparent that the skull of the *Australopithecine* fossil hominid was very similar to that of an ape. The two essential points that unify these studies thus emerged at the outset: first, that the human supralaryngeal vocal tract is species-specific and necessary for producing the full range of sounds that characterize human speech; and second, that the human vocal tract must have evolved from a form that is similar to the non-human primate.

The paper that followed showed that human newborns appeared to have the same supralaryngeal vocal tracts as non-human primates. This paper, "Newborn Infant Cry and Nonhuman Primate Vocalization", though published in 1971, was completed in 1968. It made use of the same techniques of acoustic analysis as the earlier paper. These findings on the human newborn became crucial in providing the insight that led to our reconstruction of the phonetic ability of extinct hominids like classic Neanderthal man. The reader will note that the acoustic analyses of these first two papers show that the phonetic ranges of non-human primates and newborn humans is somewhat smaller than that demonstrated in the last four papers. We developed the technique of simulating the supralaryngeal vocal tract's acoustic output to avoid the critical objection that can be addressed to any analysis of actual cries and calls. It is always possible that an animal may not make full use of the possibilities that his speech-producing anatomy provides. The experimenter might, for example, wrongly conclude that the animal was incapable of making a particular sound because the animal happened to not make the sound during the collection of data. The technique of modelling the supralaryngeal vocal tract on a digital computer avoids this problem. The experimenter can systematically explore the range of anatomical possibilities and thereby ascertain the inherent limits that the vocal tract anatomy imposes on the animal's phonetic repertoire. The results of this technique actually did not modify our earlier conclusions regarding the essential lack of shape variation in the supralaryngeal vocal tracts of non-human primates and newborn humans, except to show that vowels like $/I/$, $/e/$ and $/æ/$ can be produced by means of essentially the same tongue-articulation as the schwa vowel $/Λ/$. This is in accord with contemporary X-ray studies of adult human speech, though it is rather different from 'classic' phonetic theory (which indeed is in need of many major revisions).

It is obvious that this work has been a cooperative effort, and I would like to note my appreciation of the help that I have received from my colleagues. This work, in its later phases, would have been absolutely impossible without the insights and labors of Edmund S. Crelin, whose reconstructions of the speech-producing anatomy of fossil hominids have shed new light on the evolution of modern man. Katherine S. Harris, Dennis H. Klatt, William A. Wilson and Peter Wolff have been active collaborators who each brought their special insights and backgrounds to bear on this problem. The encouragement and comments of my colleagues at the University of

Connecticut and at Haskins Laboratories has also been invaluable, especially that of Arthur S. Abramson, Franklin S. Cooper, William S. Laughlin and Alvin M. Liberman.

## REFERENCES

Capranica, R. R.
  1965  *The Evoked Vocal Response of the Bullfrog* (Cambridge, Mass., M.I.T. Press).
Crelin, E. S., P. Lieberman, and D. H. Klatt
  Forthcoming *Anatomy and related phonetic ability of the Skhul V, Steinheim, and Rhodesian fossils and the Pleisianthropus reconstruction.*
Darwin, C.
  1871  *Descent of Man and Selection in Relation to Sex* (London, Murray).
Gardner, R. A. and B. T. Gardner
  1969  "Teaching sign language to a chimpanzee". *Science*, 165, 664-672.
Greenewalt, C. A.
  1967  *Bird Song: Acoustics and Physiology* (Washington, D.C., Smithsonian).
Hewes, G. W.
  1971  *Language Origins: A Bibliography* (Dept. of Anthropology, University of Colorado, Boulder).
Kenyon, K. W.
  1969  *The Sea Otter in the Eastern Pacific Ocean* (U.S. Govt. Printing Office).
Lenneburg, E. H.
  1967  *Biological Foundations of Language* (New York, Wiley).
Lieberman, P.
  1970  "Towards a unified phonetic theory", *Linguistic Inquiry*, 1, 307-322.
Lieberman, P. and E. S. Crelin
  1971  "On the speech of Neanderthal man", *Linguistic Inquiry*, 2, 203-222.
Lieberman, P., E. S. Crelin and D. H. Klatt
  1972  "Phonetic ability and related anatomy of newborn and adult human, Neanderthal man and chimpanzee", *American Anthropologist*, 74, 287-307.
Manly, R. S. and L. C. Braley
  1950  "Masticatory performance and efficiency", *J. Dent. Res.*, 29, 448-462.
Manly, R. S. and F. R. Shiere
  1950  "The effect of dental deficiency on mastication and food preference", *Oral Surg., Oral Med., and Oral Path*, 3, 674-685.
Manly, R. S. and P. Vinton
  1951  "A survey of the chewing ability of denture wearers", *J. Dent. Res.*, 30, 314-321.
Negus, V. E.
  1949  *The Comparative Anatomy and Physiology of the Larynx* (New York, Hafner).
Premack, D.
  1972  "Language in chimpanzee?", *Science*, 172, 808-822.

Stevens, K. N.
  1969  "The quantal nature of speech: Evidence from articulatory-acoustic data", In *Human Communication: A Unified View*, E. E. David, Jr. and P. B. Denes, eds. (New York, McGraw-Hill).
Wollberg, Z. and J. D. Newman
  1972  "Auditory cortex of squirrel monkey: Response patterns of single cells to species-specific vocalizations", *Science*, 175, 212-214.

# PRIMATE VOCALIZATIONS AND HUMAN LINGUISTIC ABILITY

PHILIP LIEBERMAN

### ABSTRACT

Some representative vocalizations of captive rhesus monkey, chimpanzee, and gorilla were recorded and analyzed by means of sound spectrograms and oscillograms. It was found that these animals' vocal mechanisms do not appear capable of producing human speech. The laryngeal output was breathy and irregular. A uniform cross section, schwalike configuration appeared to underlie all the vocalizations. These animals did not modify the shape of their supralaryngeal vocal tracts by means of tongue maneuvers during a vocalization. Formant transitions occurred in some vocalizations, but they appeared to have been generated by means of laryngeal and possibly velar or lip movements. The nonhuman primates lack a pharyngeal region like man's, where the cross-sectional area continually changes during speech. The data suggest that speech cannot be viewed as an overlaid function that makes use of a vocal tract that has evolved solely for respiratory and deglutitious purposes; the skeletal evidence of human evolution shows a series of changes from the primate vocal tract that may have been, in part, for the purpose of generating speech. Articulate speech may not have been fully developed in some of man's ancestors. The study of the peripheral speech-production apparatus of a fossil thus may be useful in the assessment of its phylogenetic grade.

## INTRODUCTION

We are accustomed to speak about the 'vocal tract' when we refer to the articulatory apparatus that is used to produce human speech. One of the most common statements about speech production, however, is that it is an 'overlaid' function insofar as it involves the manipulation of muscles and structures that have evolved for the purposes of eating and breathing. According to this view, there is, strictly speaking, no 'vocal tract'. Man has a set of devices that have evolved so that he can eat and breathe.[1, 2] He has happily been able to make use of this set of breathing and eating devices to communicate. This view, which is rather pervasive, stems from the anatomical and philosophical studies of the seventeenth and eighteenth centuries.

In the first half of the seventeenth century, Descartes[3, 4] developed his concept of the *bête machine*, i.e., animals are machines or mechanisms. In contrast to all other animals, only man possesses abstract thought and language. The basis for this distinction between man and all other animals appeared to rest solely on man's mental abilities, since animals like the apes appeared to have all the output mechanisms that are necessary for speech. Studies like Perrault's[5] and Tyson's[6] comparative anatomies of the chimpanzee showed that the larynx, teeth, lips, and jaws of the nonhuman primates were similar to those of man. However, the monkeys and apes lacked speech and language and they could not think in abstract terms. They lacked the mechanism for abstract thought, that is, they lacked language.

Since Descartes, many people have tried to show that there is no fundamental difference between man and the animals. La Mettrie[7], in *L'Homme Machine*, stated that man also was a machine. La Mettrie says that the apes are, in effect, retarded people. Since they have

---

[1]  V. E. Negus, *The Comparative Anatomy and Physiology of the Larynx*, New York, (Hafner Publishing Co., 1949).

[2]  Other factors in the evolution of man's vocal tract are also sometimes cited, e.g., erect posture and man's visual acuity, which reduced the importance of the sense of smell, is cited by Negus as the reason for the degeneration of the ability of the epiglottis to seal the mouth off from the rest of the respiratory system.

[3]  R. Descartes, *The Philosophical Works of Descartes*, E. S. Haldane and G. R. T. Ross, Trans. (New York, Dover Publications, Inc., 1955).

[4]  R. Descartes, "Correspondence", H. A. P. Torrey, Trans. in *The Philosophy of Descartes* (New York, Holt, Rinehart and Winston, Inc., 1892).

[5]  C. Perrault, *Mémoires Pour Servir à l'Histoire Naturelle des Animaux* (Paris, L'Imprimerie Royale, 1676).

[6]  E. Tyson, *Orang-outang, Sive Homo Sylvestris: or, the Anatomy of a Pygmie Compared With That of a Monkey, an Ape, and a Man* (London, Thomas Bennett and Daniel Brown, 1699). (The 1730 edition is available on microfilm from the Library of Congress.)

[7]  J. O. La Mettrie, *de L'Homme-Machine* (1747), A. Vartanian, Ed. (Princeton N. J., Princeton University Press, 1960, critical edition).

the necessary mechanism for speech production, La Mettrie believed that with a little effort it should be possible to teach an ape to talk. If an ape were carefully tutored as though he were, for example, a deaf child, it would be possible to teach him to speak. The ape would then, in La Mettrie's terms, "...be a perfect little gentleman". The belief that apes have a speech output mechanism that would be adequate for speech production has persisted to the present time. Osgood[8], for example, states that, "the chimpanzee is capable of vocalizations almost as elaborate as man's". Yerkes and Learned[9] identify more than 32 speech sounds for the chimpanzee. Attempts to teach chimpanzees to talk still continue. A recent study by Hayes[10], for example, centered about an attempt to teach a chimpanzee to talk by raising it as though it were a retarded child. No one, however, has ever been able to teach an ape to talk.

The object of this study is thus to examine the cries of nonhuman primates in order to determine what aspects of their vocalizations are similar to human speech and what aspects are different. In particular, we would like to determine the articulatory and anatomical bases of the differences so that we can tell with greater certainty the direction in which human speech-producing capability has evolved from these related animals, the apes and monkeys. In so doing, we may be able to gain some insights into the evolution of man's linguistic abilities by comparing these animals with the skeletal remains of man's ancestors. These questions are, of course, relevant to whether speech is an overlaid function, and we, of course, should be able to determine whether it is inherently possible to teach an ape to produce human speech.

## PROCEDURE

Vocalizations of captive 2- and 3-year-old gorillas (*Gorilla gorilla*),

[8]   C. E. Osgood, *Method and Theory in Experimental Psychology* (New York, Oxford University Press, 1953), 692.
[9]   R. M. Yerkes and D. W. Learned, *Chimpanzee Intelligence and its Vocal Expressions* (Baltimore, Williams and Wilkins, 1925).
[10]   C. Hayes, *The Ape in Our House* (New York, Harper & Brothers, 1952).

2-year old chimpanzees (*Pan*), and 1- to 6-year old rhesus monkeys (*Macaca mulatta*) were recorded. The range of vocalizations recorded for the rhesus monkeys was judged by their keepers to be characteristic of the animals' range. The ape vocalizations were judged by their keepers to be characteristic of a good part of these animals' 'public' range. The vocalizations furthermore are consistent with those reported by Rowell and Hinde[11] for captive rhesus monkey and by Andrew[12] for captive rhesus monkey and chimpanzee. These two studies made use of tape recordings and spectrographic analysis, so we have a reasonable basis for comparison. The cries also appear to be consistent with subjective transcriptions of ape vocalizations in their natural environment.[9-16]

Tape recordings were made in the monkey colony of the University of Connecticut at Storrs, at the Central Park and Prospect Park Zoos in New York City, and at the Fairmount Park Zoo in Philadelphia. Sony type TC 800 tape recorders were used with Sony type F85 and General Radio type 1560 P-5 microphones at a tape speed of 7.5 in./sec. The microphones were placed 5-25 cm from the monkeys. The microphone-to-mouth distances for the apes ranged from 5 cm to 8 m. The upper limit of the system's frequency response was 12 kHz. Sound spectrograms of these recordings were made, using a Voiceprint sound spectrograph. Some of the tape recordings were analyzed at half-speed and one-quarter speed to increase the effective bandwidth of the spectrograph's analyzing filter. The effective bandwidths of the analyzing filters thus ranged from 50 to 1200 Hz. Oscillograms were also made, using a Honeywell Visicorder.

[11]  T. E. Rowell and R. A. Hinde, "Vocal Communication by the Rhesus Monkey (Macaca Mulatta)", *Proc. Zoolog. Soc. London*, (1962) 138, 279-294.
[12]  R. J. Andrew, "Trends Apparent in the Evolution of Vocalization in the Old World Monkeys and Apes", *Symposium 10, The Primates* (Zoological Society of London, London, 1963), 39, 102.
[13]  R. M. Yerkes and A. W. Yerkes, *The Great Apes* (New Haven, Yale University Press, 1929).
[14]  J. Goodall, "Chimpanzees of the Gombe Stream Reserve", in *Primate Behavior*, I. DeVore, Ed. (New York, Holt, Rinehart and Winston, 1965).
[15]  V. Reynolds and F. Reynolds "Chimpanzees of the Budongo Forest", in *Primate Behavior*, I. DeVore, Ed. (New York, Holt, Rinehart and Winston, Inc., 1965).
[16]  V. Reynolds, *The Apes* (New York, E. P. Dutton and Co., 1967).

RESULTS

In Fig. 1, a wide-band spectrogram is presented of a vocalization of Gorilla Kathy, who is 3 years old and lives in Philadelphia. The gorilla was producing a signal at moderate intensity when food was withheld. The bandwidth of the analyzing filter was 300 Hz, and

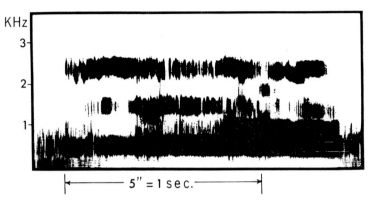

Gorilla

Fig. 1. Spectrogram of cry produced at moderate intensity by 3-year-old gorilla. The bandwidth of the analyzing filter was 300 Hz. The fundamental frequency of phonation ranged from 100 to 120 Hz. The configuration of the gorilla's supralaryngeal vocal tract apparently approximated a uniform tube open at one end, the schwa vowel, since the formant frequencies of the cry occurred at 500, 1500, and 2400 Hz. (After reduction of Figures, scale is now ⌐2.13 in. = 1 sec.)

the spectrogram was made using the FLAT position of the spectrograph, since there is more high-frequency energy in the glottal excitation of the gorilla than is the case for human vocalization. This is also the case for the chimpanzee and monkey vocalizations that are described next.

The fundamental frequency of phonation was, however, rather unstable. Large pitch perturbations[17] occurred from one period to the next. The laryngeal output appears to be very noisy and turbulent. Energy concentrations can be noted in Fig. 1 at 500, 1500, and

[17] P. Lieberman, "Perturbations in Vocal Pitch", *J. Acoust. Soc. Amer.* (1961) 33, 344-353.

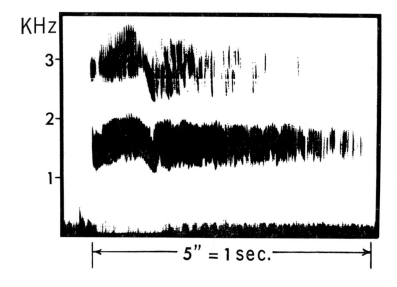

**Chimpanzee**

Fig. 2. Spectrogram of cry produced at high level of intensity by 2-year-old chimpanzee. The bandwidth of the analyzing filter was 300 Hz. Note the presence of voicing "stations" during the transitions in the initial part of the cry. The fundamental frequency of phonation is 140 Hz. The transitions thus must reflect changes in the length of the supralaryngeal vocal tract. (After reduction of Figure, scale is now ⌐3.0 in. = 1 sec.)

2400 Hz. Measurements of the skull and mandible of an adult gorilla yield an estimated vocal tract length of 17.8 cm. If a gorilla thus uttered the schwa vowel, that is, a vowel having a vocal tract shape that approximates a uniform tube open at one end, the vowel formant frequencies would be at 470, 1414, and 2355 Hz.[18] We can therefore infer that the energy concentrations in the spectrogram of gorilla Kathy's vocalization reflect the transfer function of her supralaryngeal vocal tract in the schwa configuration.

The last third of this spectrogram shows some effects that may

[18]   C. G. M. Fant, *Acoustic Theory of Speech Production* (The Hague, Mouton, 1960).

represent interaction of the supralaryngeal vocal tract with the activity of the vocal cords. We will return to these effects later. The main characteristic of this utterance is that the output of the gorilla's larynx is being modified by the resonances of the supralaryngeal vocal tract, as is the case for human speech. Note that this is in sharp contrast to the calls of birds, where the fundamental frequency and harmonics of the syrinx's output completely characterize the acoustic nature of the cry.[19]

In Fig. 2, a cry uttered by a 2-year-old chimpanzee is presented. The bandwidth of the spectrograph's analyzing filter was 300 Hz. The two energy concentrations at 1500 and 2800 Hz occur after the initial part of the vocalization where transitions to and from 1300 to 1700 to 1300 Hz and from 2800 to 3200 to 2500 Hz occur. Note the presence of clearly defined 'voicing striations' during these transitions. The fundamental frequency of phonation as determined from the oscillogram is 240 Hz. The energy concentrations that can be seen in Fig. 2 thus must reflect the transfer function of the chimpanzee's supralaryngeal vocal tract. The transitions in the initial part of Fig. 2 must reflect changes in the over-all length of the chimpanzee's vocal tract, since both $F_1$ and $F_2$ rise and fall together.

In American English, changes in the over-all length of the supralaryngeal vocal tract usually are the result of lip rounding. It is possible, however, to change the length of the vocal tract by moving the larynx up or down. Infants do this in their birth cries[20], and in some languages, e.g., certain dialects of French, laryngeal motion is a normal distinctive articulatory gesture. Since the chimpanzee's lips were retracted while he uttered this cry, he probably moved his larynx upwards and downwards to change the length of his supralaryngeal vocal tract during the early part of the utterance in Fig. 2.

Energy concentrations occurred at 1500, 2800, and 4500 Hz during the steady-state portion of this cry. The length of a chimpanzee vocal tract was estimated at 12 cm from an adult skull and mandible.

[19]   P. F. Marler and W. J. Hamilton, *Mechanisms of Animal Behavior* (New York, John Wiley & Sons, Inc., 1966).
[20]   H. M. Truby, J. F. Bosma, and J. Lind, *Newborn Infant Cry* (Uppsala, Almqvist and Wiksells, 1965).

The resonances of a uniform 12-cm tube open at both ends are 1400, 2800, and 4200 Hz. If the chimpanzee's vocal tract looked like a uniform tube, open at both ends, we would expect to find the energy concentrations that are apparent in Fig. 2. The boundary condition looking back at the subglottal system from the chimpanzee's larynx would thus have to be similar to the boundary condition at the chimpanzee's lips for this open tube approximation to hold. The chimpanzee's glottal opening would therefore have to be large during the cry for this to be true. This may be what is happening. Kelemen[21], in his anatomical study of the chimpanzee larynx, notes the presence of the 'hiatus intervocalis', that is, an opening of the glottis that is always present. This cry furthermore was produced at a high degree of vocal effort where the chimpanzee probably is using a high subglottal air pressure. In the absence of a concurrent increase in laryngeal medial compression, the vocal cords may be blown apart. These comments on what may be happening during the production of this cry are, of course, hypotheses whose confirmation or refutation is subject to further study. It is clear, however, that the chimpanzee is not changing his supralaryngeal vocal tract configuration by moving his tongue.

Figure 3 presents a cry that was produced at a low degree of vocal effort while the chimpanzee was eating. The bandwidth of the analyzing filter of the spectrograph was 300 Hz. The cry consists of two bursts about 300 msec apart. The fundamental frequency of phonation as measured on the oscillogram was 150 Hz during the first burst and 210 Hz during the second burst. A quantized spectrogram was used to determine the spectral energy concentrations of the cry. Energy concentrations occurred at 650, 1650, and 3100 Hz. The chimpanzee's lips were rounded throughout this cry. This would make the chimpanzee's supralaryngeal vocal tract somewhat longer than it was in the cry presented in Fig. 2, where his lips were retracted. If his vocal tract approximated a 13 cm long uniform tube open at one end, we would expect formant frequencies at 620, 1860, and 3100 Hz. $F_1$ is somewhat higher and $F_2$ is somewhat lower. The

[21]   G. Kelemen, "The Anatomical Basis of Phonation in the Chimpanzee", *J. Morphol.* (1948) 82, 229-256.

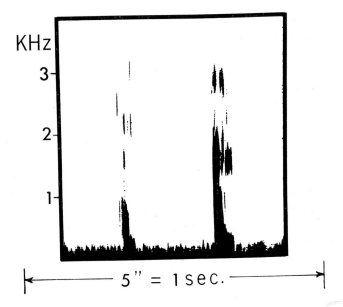

## Chimpanzee

Fig. 3. Spectrogram of cry produced at low degree of vocal effort by 2-year chimpanzee. The bandwidth of the analyzing filter was 300 Hz. The fundamental frequency was 150 and 210 Hz, respectively, for the two "bursts". The formant frequencies occurred at 650, 1650, and 3100 Hz. The chimpanzee's supralaryngeal vocal tract thus approximated a slightly flared uniform tube open at one end. (After reduction of Figure, scale is now ⌐3.25 in. = 1 sec.)

chimpanzee's supralaryngeal vocal tract is thus somewhat flared.[22]

Note that the cry at a low effort, where the glottal opening is probably small, has formants corresponding to a quarter-wave resonator. The cry at a high degree of effort, where the glottal opening is perhaps large, apparently results in the formants corresponding to a half-wave resonator. The crucial point is that in both cases, the shape of the supralaryngeal vocal tract seems to approximate a uni-

---

[22]   K. N. Stevens, "The Quantal Nature of Speech: Evidence from Articulatory-Acoustic Data", in *Human Communication: A Unified View*, E. E. David, Jr., and P. B. Denes, Eds. (New York, McGraw-Hill Book Co.).

form tube, that is, the schwa vowel. In all of the analyses of the ape cries that we recorded, the acoustic signal indicated that the supralaryngeal vocal tract configuration approximated either a tube of uniform cross section or a slightly flared tube. The data sample is admittedly small, as it involves only six captive apes, but the cries recorded are consistent with Andrew's spectrographic investigation.[23]

In several subjective studies of ape cries[9, 13], transcriptions like /aw/ are used for certain cries. This, of course, implies that the ape is moving his tongue during the cry since this is what human speakers do when they produce the diphthong /aw/. In Fig. 4, a spectrogram is presented of a chimpanzee cry that sounds like /aw/. The cry was uttered at a high degree of vocal effort. The fundamental

[23]  Rowell and Hinde (note 11) used narrow-bandwidth spectrograms. This makes it difficult to compare our data directly with the cries presented in his study, since it is difficult to deduce vocal tract configurations from narrow-bandwidth spectrograms. Narrow-bandwidth spectrograms are appropriate for the analysis of bird calls, where the acoustic characteristics of the signal are structured in terms of the fundamental frequency and harmonic structure of the excitation function (the output of the syrinx). They are insufficient, however, when the acoustic characteristics of the signal are determined in part by the transfer function of the supralaryngeal vocal tract's configuration, which acts as an acoustic filter on the excitation function. The exclusive use of narrow-bandwidth spectrograms can lead to descriptions that, although acoustically valid in terms of the narrow-bandwith analysis, are inappropiate in terms of the acoustically and perceptually significant aspects of the signal. Marler and Hamilton (note 19), for example, note that, "Compared with the calls of birds, many sounds used by primates and other mammals are coarse, lacking the purity of tone and precise patterns of frequency modulation that occur in many passerine bird songs". This statement is true insofar as the primates do not produce cries that can be described in terms of one or two 'pure' sinusoidal components. Yet neither can human speech be described in terms of one or two pure tones, "... or precise patterns of frequency modulation ...". If the methodology that is appropriate for the analysis of bird calls were used for the analysis of human speech it would be extremely difficult to isolate most of the significant phonologic elements. We would perhaps conclude that human speech employed, 'coarse' sounds, i.e., sounds that were not inherently musical. The point here is, of course, that the acoustic analysis must be appropriate for the signal. In order to investigate the effects of the supralaryngeal vocal tract, we must use analyzing filters that have a bandwidth sufficient to encompass two or more harmonics of the excitation function. This aspect of speech analysis is discussed in detail by W. Koenig, H. K. Dunn, and L. Y. Lacy, "The Sound Spectrograph", *J. Acoust-Soc. Amer.* (1946) 17, 19-49.

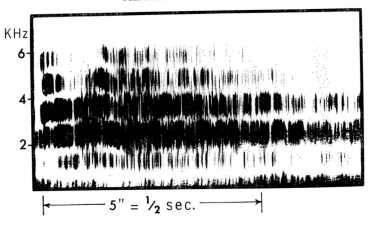

## Chimpanzee

Fig. 4. Spectrogram of loud chimpanzee cry that sounds like diphthong /aw/. The bandwidth of the analyzing filter was 600 Hz. Note the decrease in the high-frequency energy of the glottal excitation that is apparent in the change in density in the second, third, and fourth 'bars' towards the end of the cry. Note that there are *no* transitions involving the first and second formants. The ape's tongue thus did not change the shape of this supralaryngeal vocal tract. (After reduction of Figure, scale is now ⌐2.4 in. = ½ sec.)

frequency was unstable. The oscillogram showed that it varied about 200 Hz, but the excitation was, in general, very breathy. The sound spectrogram in Fig. 4 was made with an analyzing filter bandwidth of 600 Hz by analyzing the tape recording at half-speed. The time scale of the spectrogram is thus stretched. Note that the energy in the higher formants decreases towards the end of the cry. Note, however, that the formants continue to be evenly spaced at the end of the cry. There is no transition in either the first- or the second-formant frequencies. The apparent change in vowel quality in this cry is thus due to a change in the energy content of the glottal excitation, rather than to a change in the configuration of the supra-laryngeal vocal tract. In other words, the cry sounds like /aw/ because the energy balance between the higher and the lower formant frequencies shifts to the lower formant frequencies as the spectral content of the glottal excitation shifts towards the end of the cry.

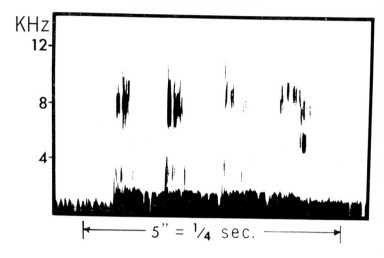

Rhesus Monkey

Fig. 5. Spectrogram of aggressive 'bark' of rhesus monkey. The bandwidth of the analyzing filter was 1200 Hz. Formant frequencies occurred at 1, 3, and 6-8 kHz. (After reduction of Figure, scale is now ⌣2.8 in. = ¼ sec.)

Similar though less pronounced changes in the spectral content of the glottal excitation can be seen in human vocalizations at the end of voicing, and in particular, at the end of a breath group, where the larynx is moving towards its open inspiratory configuration while the subglottal air pressure simultaneously falls.[24]

In Fig. 5, a spectrogram of one of the aggressive sounds of a rhesus monkey is presented. The cry was produced at a moderate degree of vocal effort while the monkey bared his teeth. We recorded six normal monkeys over a period of 6 months in the monkey colony of the University of Connecticut at Storrs. This particular recording was made with the Sony type F85 microphone. In Fig. 6, part of the oscillogram of this cry is presented. The first two 'bursts' are presented in the oscillogram that was made as the tape recording was played back at one-quarter speed. The fundamental frequency

[24]  P. Lieberman, *Intonation, Perception, and Language* (Cambridge, Mass., The MIT Press, 1967).

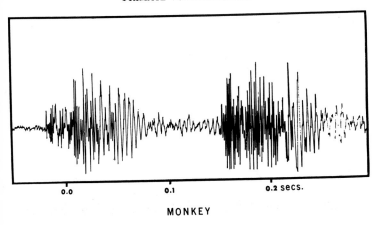

**MONKEY**

Fig. 6. Oscillogram of same utterance as Fig. 5. The tape recording was played at one-quarter speed. The fundamental frequency of phonation was about 400 Hz. The waveform resembles that characteristic of extremely hoarse human vocalization.

of phonation is approximately 400 Hz. Note that the fundamental periodicity is very unstable at best. Parts of the waveform appear to be very turbulent. The waveform, in all, looks very much like those associated with pathologic human larynges where a hoarse vocal output results.[25] The rhesus monkeys, like the gorillas and chimpanzees, are unable to produce sustained vocalizations that have a steady fundamental periodicity.

The spectrogram in Fig. 5 was also made from a tape which was played back at one-quarter speed. The effective bandwidth of the spectrograph was thus 1200 Hz. Energy concentrations occurred at 1, 3, and 6-8 kHz. There were approximately 25 msec between each burst and glottal activity seems to have been sustained between each burst .Thus, the cry is similar to a sequence of voiced stops in intervocalic position.

Unlike voiced stops in human speech, the closure of the vocal tract seems to have been effected by the animal's epiglottis and velum. The monkey's lips were retracted, exposing his teeth through-

[25] P. Lieberman, "Some Acoustic Measures of the Fundamental Periodicity of Normal and Pathologic Larynges", *J. Acoust. Soc. Amer.* (1963) 35, 344-353.

out the cry, so he could not have used his lips to obstruct his vocal tract. There are also no formant transitions, which would occur if the supralaryngeal vocal tract were momentarily obstructed by the tongue. The larynx of a rhesus monkey is quite high in contrast to the position of the human vocal tract, and his epiglottis can seal his mouth off at the soft palate.[26]

Note that this cry is quite similar to the chimpanzee cry in Fig. 3, except that it is scaled up in frequency. The energy concentrations at 2, 3 and 6-8 kHz are again consistent with the resonances of a uniform tube open at one end. We anesthetized a 5-year-old male monkey and measured the length of his supralaryngeal vocal tract. With his lips rounded, the length of his supralaryngeal vocal tract was 7.6 cm. The resonances of a uniform 7.6-cm-long tube open at one end are 1100, 3300, and 5500 Hz. We recorded a number of cries that this monkey made with his lips rounded at a low level of vocal effort. The recordings were made in a quiet room using the General Radio 1560-P5 microphone. The average values of $F_1$, $F_2$, and $F_3$ were 1300, 3000, and 4400 Hz, respectively. Thus, the monkey was producing these cries with a slightly flared supralaryngeal vocal tract.

In Fig. 7, photographs of a casting of the oral cavity of a rhesus monkey are presented. The monkey's tongue and lips were positioned in an approximation of an aggressive 'bark'[11] and a plaster-of-Paris casting was made shortly after an experiment in which the monkey was sacrificed (for other purposes). Note that the vocal tract of the monkey approximates a uniform cross section passage with a flared portion at the laryngeal end. Also note the shallowness of the pharyngeal 'bend' and the flatness of the monkey's tongue, which is apparent in the side view. (The monkey's tongue fills up the shallow section delimited by the depth of the 'bend' at the laryngeal end of the oral cavity.)

In Fig. 8, a distress cry of a rhesus monkey is presented. This cry was produced at an extremely high level of vocal effort. The mon-

---

[26]   F. D. Geist, "Nasal Cavity, Larynx, Mouth, and Pharynx", in *Anatomy of the Rhesus Monkey*, C. G. Hartman, Ed. (New York, Hafner Publishing Co., 1961).

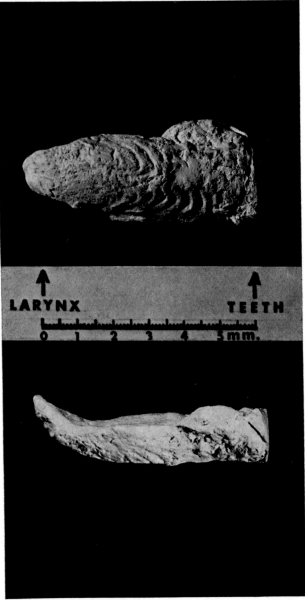

Fig. 7. Side and top views of a casting of the oral cavity of an adult rhesus monkey. The monkey's tongue and lips were positioned in an approximation of an aggressive 'bark'. Note the uniform cross section of most of the oral cavity.

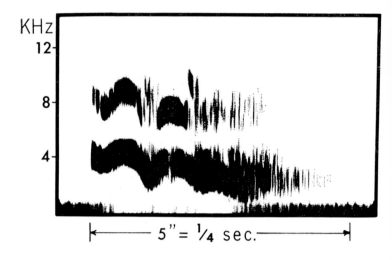

## Rhesus Monkey

Fig. 8. Spectrogram of distress cry of rhesus monkey. The bandwidth of the analyzing filter was 1200 Hz, The waveform of this cry shows that energy is present at only the resonances of the monkey's supralaryngeal vocal tract during the initial part of the cry. (After reduction of Figure, scale is now ⌣2.8 in. = ¼ sec.)

key had its lips retracted. It was clinging to the back of another monkey at the rear of its cage. The bandwidth of the spectrograph filter was 1200 Hz, since the tape recording was analyzed at one-quarter speed. Note the energy concentrations in the initial part of this vocalization. The supraglottal vocal tract length of this monkey is about 4 cm when his lips are fully retracted and he is anesthetized. The lowest energy concentration ranges from 4 to 4.5 kHz during the initial part of the cry. This frequency range is consistent with a 4-cm vocal tract length resonating as a half-wave resonator. The next highest energy concentration ranges from 8.5 to 9 kHz during the initial part of the cry. This too is consistent with the second resonance of a uniform tube that has similar boundary conditions at both ends. There is no low-frequency fundamental frequency apparent in the initial part of this cry. Examination of the oscillogram shows energy present only at the two resonances of the supralaryngeal vocal tract. We have here a case where the resonances of the supralaryngeal vocal tract apparently control the excitation function. In other words, the resonances of the vocal tract determine the energy components of the laryngeal excitation. The system is behaving like a trumpet where the resonances of the trumpet determine the rate at which the musician's lips vibrate. Similar though smaller effects have been noted during normal human speech where the vocal cords can be seen to vibrate at the first formant frequency.[27] Flanagan has observed similar effects [28] in a model of the human larynx. In the gorilla cry in Fig. 1, energy can be seen at multiples of the first formant during the last third of the spectrogram. The abrupt 'bars' may be caused by the vocal cords of the gorilla vibrating at the first formant frequency. Similar effects also seem to occur in human speech from dysarthric subjects.[29]

Returning to Fig. 8, note that the energy concentrations at the end of the cry are at 2.5 and 7 kHz. These frequencies are consistent with a flared 4-cm tube resonating as a quarter-wave resonator. Note that there is less energy in the high part of the spectrum at the end of the cry. The oscillogram also shows low-frequency energy and a general noiselike to quasiperiodic nature where the fundamental frequency is about 600 Hz. The monkey's vocal tract apparently resembles a half-wave resonator during the initial part of the cry where the higher subglottal air pressure produces a large glottal opening. During the final part of the cry, the lower subglottal air pressure probably results in a smaller average glottal opening that results in resonances in the quarter-wave mode.

The cry in Fig. 8, which we have been discussing, is consistent

[27] H. I. Soron, Air Force Cambridge Research Laboratories, has noted these effects in high-speed motion pictures of the human vocal cords during phonation.

[28] J. L. Flanagan, "Acoustic Properties of Vocal Sound Sources", *Proc. Conf. Sound Production in Man* (New York, New York Acad. Sci., 1968).

[29] K. S. Harris, Haskins Laboratories, New York (private communication).

with the distress cries[30, 31] recorded by Andrew[12] and by Rowell and Hinde.[11] Andrew, for example, notes that these cries have no energy below 2 kHz in contrast to the other cries he recorded. This is probably due to the coupling between the supralaryngeal vocal tract and the larynx. The monkey whose cry is presented in Fig. 8 has a vocal tract length that is half that of most adult monkeys, which accounts for the fact that no energy occurs below 4 kHz. The movements of the formants that also characterize these cries are due to the vertical movement of the monkey's larynges.

## DISCUSSION

The cries of the nonhuman primates are similar to human speech insofar as they are produced by exciting a supralaryngeal vocal tract with glottal and noise sources. In bird calls, the output of the syrinx determines the acoustic quality of the cry, but for the nonhuman primates, as for man, the character of the acoustic signal is determined by the source and the supralaryngeal vocal tract, which acts as an acoustic filter. Our data indicate, however, that the nonhuman primates would not be capable of producing human speech even if

[30] One last comment should be made concerning these distress cries. When one listens to these cries played back at their normal speed, they sound like birdlike chirps. There is no sense of fright or terror. However, when the signals are scaled down in frequency by playing the tapes at one-quarter speed, the cries convey extreme fright. Darwin's theory (C. Darwin, *The Expression of Emotion in Man and Animals* [London, J. Murray, 1872]) of the innate expression of emotion through the vocal mechanism would seem to be correct. We do not normally interpret the rhesus monkey's fright cries correctly when we hear them, because the output mechanism of the rhesus monkey produces an acoustic signal that is scaled up in frequency relative to our range. When we hear the cry scaled down in frequency we are able to interpret it. The motor controls to the rhesus monkey's vocal mechanism when it expresses fright are probably similar to the motor controls that we would use, but the acoustic signal has been scaled up in frequency because the rhesus monkey is much smaller. When we play back the tape at one-quarter speed, we match the acoustic signal to our own perceptual recognition routines, which appear to be structured in terms of the constraints of our own speech-production mechanism; see also Ref. 31.

[31] A. M. Liberman, F. S. Cooper, K. S. Harris and P. F. MacNeilage, "A Motor Theory of Speech Perception", *Proc. Speech Communication Seminar* (Stockholm, Speech Transmission Laboratory, Royal Inst. Tech., 1962).

they had the requisite mental ability. Unlike man, the nonhuman primates do *not* appear to change the shape of their supralaryngeal vocal tracts by moving their tongues during the production of a cry.[32] The only vocal-tract shape that the monkeys and apes use is one similar to a slightly /a/-like schwa, i.e., a slightly flared uniform

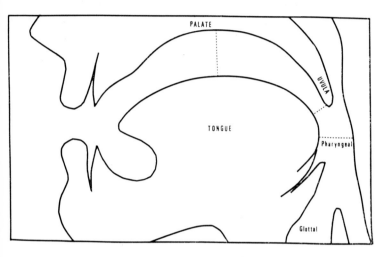

Fig. 9. Schematized view of the human oral and pharyngeal region. Note the relative thickness of the tongue. The anterior wall of the pharynx in man is formed by the tongue and the cross-sectional area of this back cavity can vary over a ten-to-one range. A variable pharyngeal region is essential for the production of back vowels and consonants.

tube. The phonetic quality of human speech, in contrast, involves the continual modification of the shape of the supralaryngeal vocal tract by the tongue.

In Fig. 9, a schematized view of the pharyngeal and oral regions

[32]   J. Bastian, "Primate Signaling Systems and Human Languages", in *Primate Behavior: Field Studies of Monkeys and Apes*, I. Devore, Ed. (New York, Holt, Rinehart and Winston, Inc., 1965) notes that the auditory signals of humans and primates have certain similarities, but that the "... disposition of the parts of the filtering system remains rather stable during signal emission.... Most of the departures from the relatively stable and open configurations occur at the beginnings of signals and appear to be most often due to the involvement of open parts at the very front (the lips) or the very back ...."

of the human supralaryngeal vocal tract is presented. Note that the anterior wall of the pharyngeal region is formed by the back of the tongue. The human tongue is thick in comparison with its length. The shape of the pharyngeal region constantly changes during the production of human speech as the tongue moves backwards and forwards. The cross-sectional area of the pharynx varies, for example, over a ten-to-one range for the vowels /a/ and /i/. The vowel /a/ is produced with a small pharyngeal cross section, while the /i/ is produced with a large cross section. These variations in pharyngeal

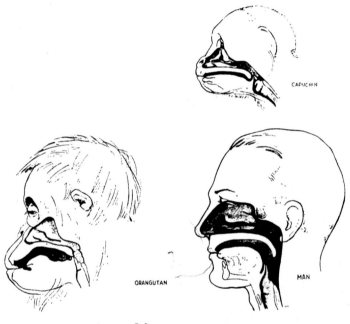

by Negus

Fig. 10. Semidiagrammatic representation of the nose, palate, tongue, pharynx and larynx of a monkey and of man from Negus' *Comparative Anatomy and Physiology of the Larynx*. Note the relative position of the palate and larynx in the two diagrams. The monkey lacks a pharyngeal region whose anterior wall can move. The monkey cannot change the configuration of his supralaryngeal vocal tract by means of a thick mobile tongue.

cross-sectional area are characteristic for consonants as well as vowels and they are essential in the production of human speech.

In Fig. 10, a semidiagrammatic representation of the nose, palate, tongue, pharynx, and larynx of a monkey, an ape, and man are reproduced from Negus' *Comparative Anatomy and Physiology of the Larynx*.[1] Note the relative positions of the palate and larynx. The basis for the nonhuman primates' lack of tongue mobility appears to be anatomical. The pharyngeal region, which can vary its shape in man, has no real counterpart in these animals. Their larynges are positioned quite high compared to the human larynx, almost in line with the roof of the palate. The tongues of these animals are thin compared to man's. The nonhuman primates do not have a pharynx where the root of a thick tongue forms a movable anterior wall. Zhinkin,[33] for example, in a cineradiographic study of baboon cries, shows that the baboon can not vary the size of his pharynx. The tongues of the nonhuman primates are long and flat and their supralaryngeal vocal tracts cannot assume the range of shape changes characteristic of human speech.

In Fig. 11, we have reproduced a second illustration from Negus. Negus[1] notes that there has been a continuing set of changes in the evolution of the upper respiratory system. He notes, for example, that Neanderthal man has "...no large pharyngeal resonator, as in modern man" and that "...the gap between the palate and the epiglottis has increased during evolutionary changes to that of modern man" (p. 195). If one examines the skulls of earlier hominoid fossils, like the one that Dart[34] referred to as *Australopithecus pro-*

---

[33]   N. I. Zhinkin, "An Application of the Theory of Algorithms to the Study of Animal Speech—Methods of Vocal Intercommunication between Monkeys", in *Acoustic Behavior of Animals*, R. G. Busnel, Ed. (Amsterdam, Elsevier Publishing Company, 1963).

[34]   R. A. Dart, "The Makapansgat Proto-Human *Australopithecus Prometheus*", *Am. J. Phys. Anthropol.* (1948) 6, 259-283. Dart and Broom and Schepers (R. Broom and G. W. H. Schepers, "The South African Ape-Men: the Australopithecinae", in *Transvaal Museum Memoirs*, No. 2, Pretoria, 1952) ascribe the ability to use speech to fossil anthropoids of this type. Their evidence rests on endocranial casts of these fossils from which they infer the presence of a well-developed center for the motor control of speech. Dart, "The Predatory Implemental Technique of Australopithecus", *Am. J. Phys. Anthropol.* [1949] 7, 1-38

*metheus*, the similarity between these phylogenetically primitive hominids and present day nonhuman primates is quite apparent. A plaster cast of the reconstructed skull of *Australopithecus prometheus* was compared with a chimpanzee skull. The over-all lengths of both skulls were approximately 18 cm. The shape of the mandible and the palate, and the position of the foramen magnum relative to the palate, were very similar. The mandibles of both the chimpanzee and *Australopithecus* left room for only a relatively thin tongue. The length of the supralaryngeal vocal tract was estimated to be approximately 12 cm for both specimens. Insofar as both vocal tracts would reflect the gross skeletal similarities that exist between *Australopithecus* and a modern chimpanzee, they both would lack a variable pharyngeal area. *Australopithecus* is thus in line with the evolutionary changes in the pharyngeal region that Negus notes. The earlier the fossil, the smaller the pharyngeal region is. *Australopithecus prometheus*, in all likelihood, could not have produced human speech, since his vocal apparatus, insofar as we are able to make deductions from fossil remains, appears to be quite similar to those of presentday apes and monkeys. Man's closer ancestors may or may not have been able to produce the full range of human speech. Vallois,[35] in his survey of skeletal evidence, cites the difficulties that have beset past attempts to infer the presence or absence of speech from anatomical arguments. These past difficulties were due primarily to the lack of a quantitative acoustic

---

also ascribes the use of clubs to these anthropoids. However, the use of implements has no direct connection with linguistic ability. Chimpanzees[14-16] in their natural state also use clubs and throw stones. Dart, in a later work and D. Craig, *Adventures with the Missing Link* (New York, Harper & Brothers, [1959] indeed takes note of the possibility that a primitive culture might not require linguistic ability. He notes that, "... the basic discoveries of the osteodontokeratic culture, once made by *Australopithecus*, persisted throughout human cultures until superseded, and then only in part, by the successive discoveries of stone and metals" (p. 224). He concludes that by this criterion, very little cultural change occurred until recent times and that "articulate speech came only about 25 000 years ago and was preceded by about a million years of gesture and babble" (p. 224).

[35] H. V. Vallois, "The Social Life of Early Man: The Evidence of Skeletons", *Yearbook Phys. Anthropol.* (1953-1961) 9, 110-131 and *Social Life in Early Man*, S. L. Washburn, Ed. (1961) 214-235.

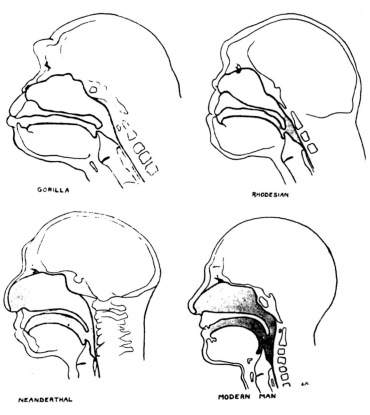

# by Negus

Fig. 11. The evolution of the vocal tract, from Negus's *Comparative Anatomy and Physiology of the Larynx*. Note the changes towards the vocal tract of modern man. The larynx has descended and a pharyngeal region that can change its cross-sectional area has developed. The earliest hominids, e.g., *Australopithecus prometheus*, had supralaryngeal vocal tracts that resemble those of the present-day nonhuman primates. They thus could not have articulated human speech.

theory of speech production, so that the interpretation of the acoustic consequences of anatomical structures was tenuous at best.

The evolution of the vocal tract thus reflects, in part, its role in speech production. Speech cannot be simply regarded as an overlaid function that makes use of a mechanism that has evolved solely for the purposes of eating and breathing. The apes and monkeys have no difficulty in either breathing or eating. In fact, they have better breathing systems than ours. The monkeys and most apes can, for example, seal their mouths off from the rest of the respiratory system because the high position of the larynx in these animals allows the epiglottis to close the mouth. The results of comparative anatomy indeed demonstrate that the role of the epiglottis is to close the mouth.[1, 2] A dog or a monkey can breathe while its mouth is full of food or water. The low position of the larynx in man also leads to difficulties when food is lodged in the larynx. This often can have fatal consequences. In no sense is the human larynx optimal for the purposes of respiration. Negus[1], for example, also shows that in contrast with the larynges of animals like the horse, the human larynx impedes the flow of air during respiration. Whereas the maximum opening of the larynx during respiration in a horse is greater than the area of the trachea, in man the maximum laryngeal area is only half of the tracheal area.

The cries of the nonhuman primates also differ from human speech insofar as the output of the larynx is less periodic. The glottal period often varies from one period to the next. In other words, large pitch perturbations[17] often occur. At high levels of effort, the output of the larynx often appears to be quite noisy and the waveform of the acoustic signal recorded from the animal resembles a tuned circuit excited by bursts of wide-band noise. In some of the very loud cries, the laryngeal output seems to be coupled to the resonances of the supralaryngeal vocal tract and energy appears to be present only at the formant frequencies. Although similar interactions between the laryngeal output and the supralaryngeal vocal tract occur in human speech, they play a very small part in normal speech production.

The differences between the nonhuman and human laryngeal output again appear to have an anatomical basis. Kelemen[21,36 – 38], in

[36]　G. Kelemen, "Physiology of Phonation in Primates", *LOGOS* (1958) 1, 32-35.

a series of detailed anatomical studies, has noted a number of differences between human and nonhuman larynges, although the larynges of all primates are superficially similar. One difference, which probably accounts, in part, for breathy excitation, is the presence of what Kelemen terms the 'hiatus intervocalis' in the nonhuman primate larynx. The animal's larynx cannot be completely adducted, and a glottal shunt always exists. The differences in the outputs of the nonhuman and human larynges may of course be due to differences in the ability to control the larynx by making fine adjustments of the tensions of the laryngeal muscles. Nevertheless, it is clear that these differences are connected with vocalization rather than with respiration.

## COMMENTS

### Linguistic Abilities of Apes and Monkeys

It is not always clear from the acoustic data of this paper what the monkeys and apes were doing when they produced their cries. The acoustic analysis indicates that some of the cries were made while the animal changed the over-all length of his supralaryngeal vocal tract by either lip rounding or by moving his larynx up and down. Some of the interrupted cries seem to have been made by the animal's closing his epiglottis and/or his velum, and in some of the cries, the vocal tract may have been behaving more like a half-wave, rather than a quarter-wave resonator. What is clear, however, from the acoustic and anatomical data is (1) that these animals do not move their tongues during a cry, and (2) that the laryngeal output tends to be aperiodic. These animals could not produce human speech even if they had the requisite mental ability. Their vocal apparatus is not adapted for the production of human speech;

---

[37] G. Kelemen and J. Sade, "The Vocal Organ of the Howling Monkey (Alouatta palliata)", *J. Morphol.* (1960) 107, 123-140.
[38] G. Kelemen, "Anatomy of the Larynx as a Vocal Organ: Evolutionary Aspects", *LOGOS* (1961) 4, 46-55.

; laryngeal control and a pharyngeal region capable of vary-
ross-sectional area.

## Evolution of the Human Vocal Mechanism

Although we can say nothing about the larynx of man's immediate
ancestors, we can see the evolution of a variable pharyngeal area
from the skeletal evidence.[1,39-41] Insofar as the presence of an output mechanism is a necessary condition for human language, and
insofar as the phonologic features have an abstract as well as a physical basis in language[42], we can say that the earliest hominid beings
did not have language. The evolution of the vocal tract seems to
move consistently towards the mechanism of modern-day man, as
we proceed from one phylogenetic grade to the next. We do not find
any 'puzzling regressions' like those that occur when one attempts
to correlate 'cosmetic' aspects of anatomy like brow ridges with
phylogenetic grade.[43]

## Man's Acquisition of Language

It is not clear exactly when language came into being. If the arguments advanced by Dart[34] concerning the long static period in the
development of human culture are valid, then the acquisition of
speech may be comparatively recent. Dart claims that man's culture
was static from the time of the *Australopithecines* to about 25,000
years ago. If the level of culture were an index of whether language
was necessary or not we could conclude that either all hominids
from the *Australopithecines* onwards had speech, or that all these
hominids lacked speech. Since *Australopithecus prometheus* proba-

---

[39]   A. Keith, *The Antiquity of Man* (London, Williams and Norgate, 1915).
[40]   W. W. Howells, Jr., *Mankind So Far* (New York, Doubleday & Company,
Inc., Garden City, 1944).
[41]   E. L. DuBrul, *Evolution of the Speech Apparatus* (Springfield, Illinois,
Charles C. Thomas, 1958).
[42]   M. Halle and N. Chomsky, *The Sound Pattern of English* (New York, Harper and Row, 1968).
[43]   C. S. Coon, *The Origin of Races* (New York, Alfred A. Knopf, Inc., 1966).

bly did not have the ability to produce speech, we would therefore conclude that none of these hominids had speech. However, Dart's statement about the presence of a static culture until 25,000 years ago fails to take into account changes in toolmaking techniques that occurred in the lower paleolithic era, that is about 100,000 years ago. Dart also probably places too much importance on the presence of language in the development of culture. Although it is quite likely that an accelerated pace of cultural change at some period reflects the presence of language, which extends man's powers of abstract thought, other factors probably are always involved. Barnett[44], for example, notes the effects of intercultural contact on cultural change. The presence of language may therefore be only a necessary rather than a sufficient factor in man's cultural development. If we take the level of culture above the *Australopithecine* baseline as an index of the presence of language, it is clear that human speech was already present by the upper paleolithic era.

We cannot, on the basis of skeletal evidence, tell exactly when human speech first appeared. We cannot, for example, state with certainty whether Neanderthal man, who is a comparatively recent hominid, could or could not have articulated the full range of human speech. This is because we cannot determine the relationship between skeletal structure and soft tissue with the detail that would be necessary to justify a positive conclusion. We also do not even know the range of vocal tract dimensions that holds for the modern man, nor do we know to what extent small differences in the vocal tract are mirrored in the acoustic signal. Other motor skills that we cannot infer from skeletal evidence, like the ability to execute the rapid, controlled articulatory maneuvers that are typical for consonants, are also necessary for the production of speech. Thus, while we can say with reasonable certainty that older fossil hominids did not possess human speech, the nearer the vocal apparatus of a fossil is to that of modern man, the greater is our uncertainty regarding his ability to produce human speech. This uncertainty merely reflects the fact that, at the present time, we know some of the factors

[44] H. G. Barnett, *Innovation: The Basis of Cultural Change* (New York, Mc-Graw-Hill Book Co., 1953).

that are necessary for the production of human speech, but we do not know what peripheral mechanisms and central controls would be sufficient for the production of human speech.

## Cries versus Language

The acquisition of language probably was an abrupt thing that came when the number of calls and cries that could be made with the available vocal mechanism increased to the point where it was more efficient to code features. We can speculate at a process in which the ability to make more and more cries gradually developed. The differentiated cries allowed the species to compete more successfully and mutations that led to the ability to make more cries were therefore retained. At some point, the number of different cries that could be made increased markedly; perhaps the mobility of the pharynx increased to the point where the phonologic features of *Back* tongue position and *High* tongue position could be produced.[42] If the computational abilities of the species were sufficiently advanced, it would have been efficient to recode the phonologic features leading to an arbitrary relationship between sound and meaning.

The difference between a system of cries, even though it may be highly developed, and a language, is that the relationship between meaning and sounds is fixed for cries. A high pitched /a/, for example, may be the cry for pain. It always 'means' pain no matter what sounds precede or follow it. In contrast, the sound /a/ in a language may have no meaning in itself, nor might the sounds /m/ or /n/ in isolation. The sound sequence /man/ does have a particular semantic reference or meaning in English while the sound sequences /ma/ and /an/ have other meanings. Language essentially involves a two-level process where it is necessary to interpose the rules of a grammar and a dictionary between the sound sequence and its meaning.

## Matching of Speech Production and Speech Perception

The two necessary conditions for the presence of speech and language, an output mechanism and central mental ability, may have developed together. Certainly everything that comes to mind about language seems to show this kind of optimization between output and internal computation. The simultaneous evolution of a mechanism for the production of speech and of man's mental ability would, for example, account for the close relationship that we find between speech production and speech perception. It would have been 'natural' and 'economical' for the constraints of speech production to be structured into the speech perception system if both of these abilities developed at the same pace. We would thus expect to find the speech recognition routines that involved a match with the constraints of speech production (the motor theory of speech perception[31]) to be structured into a speech perception center that would be species-specific, rather than in the peripheral or central auditory systems, which probably are similar for man and other animals.

### CONCLUSION

Man has apparently developed special modifications of his vocal tract for the purposes of speech production. Just as an ability to use tools depends, in part, on having an opposable thumb and an upright posture, the ability to talk depends on our having a mouth, tongue, larynx, and pharynx that are adapted towards speech production. Speech production is thus not an overlaid function that makes use of a mechanism that has evolved solely for the purposes of eating and breathing. The apes and monkeys lack the adaptations that are essential for the production of human speech and they obviously have no difficulties in either breathing or eating. Human infants, in a sense, begin at the same point as the nonhuman primates. They do not move their tongues during a cry for the first weeks of life.[45] By the sixth week of life, however, they begin to change the

[45]   Newborn human infants begin by making cries in which their tongues are immobile. They thus start by making cries that are similar to those made by the nonhuman primates. See the forthcoming study by P. Lieberman, K. S. Harris, and P. Wolff, "Newborn Infant Cry in Relation to Nonhuman Primate Vocalizations", *J. Acoust. Soc. Amer.* (1968) 44, 365(A).

configurations of their supralaryngeal vocal tracts during a vocalization. The nonhuman primates never reach this point, though their general mental ability and physical dexterity are equivalent to, or better than, a human infant's at this age.[16] Man's remote ancestors also lacked the output mechanism that is necessary for the production of speech and man may have acquired speech and speech-adapted mechanisms at a comparatively recent time. We cannot say very much about the evolution of the central mechanisms that are necessary for speech and language, but looking at the 'speech' abilities of present-day monkeys and apes gives us some insights into the nature, the evolution, and the acquisition of man's linguistic ability.

## ACKNOWLEDGMENTS

Thanks are due to Ronald Ellis and Kenneth Welch of the Prospect Park Zoo, Brooklyn, New York, and John Fitzgerald of the Central Park Zoo, New York City, and Dr. W. A. Wilson of the University of Connecticut for their aid in recording their charges. Special thanks are also due to Miss Carolyn Ristau of the University of Pennsylvania who made her tape recordings of apes available. The acoustic analysis has also profited from the special insights of Dr. Franklin S. Cooper of Haskins Laboratories, while the interpretation of anthropological theories has benefited from the advice of Dr. D. J. Nash of the University of Connecticut and Dr. L. C. Eiseley of the University of Pennsylvania. This research was supported in substantial part by grants from the National Institute of Child Health and Human Development and the National Institute of Dental Research.

# NEWBORN INFANT CRY AND NONHUMAN-PRIMATE VOCALIZATIONS

PHILIP LIEBERMAN[1], KATHERINE S.HARRIS[2]
PETER WOLFF[3] AND LORRAINE H. RUSSELL[4]

## ABSTRACT

Cries were recorded from 20 normal newborn infants from birth to the fourth day of life. Sound spectrograms showed that these cries were similar to the vocalizations of non-human primates insofar as the infants seemed to produce these sounds by means of a uniform cross-section, schwa-like, vocal tract configuration. Under certain conditions the laryngeal excitation was breathy and the formant frequencies corresponding to an open boundary condition at the glottis were generated. The infants did not produce the range of sounds typical of adult human speech. This inability appears to reflect, in part, limitations imposed by the neonatal vocal apparatus, which resembles the non-human primate vocal tract insofar as it appears to be inherently incapable of producing the full range of human speech. The initial restrictions on the soundmaking repertoire of human infants are also evident in previous perceptually based transcriptions of the utterances of infants as well as in spectrographic and cineradiographic studies.

It is possible to differentiate at least three stages in the acquisition of speech by children: cry, babble and word acquisition. The object of this study is to examine the earliest stage of infant cry, that is, neonatal cry. We shall attempt to relate our results to previous cineradiographic, acoustic, and perceptual studies of infant cry and to the latter stages of language acquisition. We shall also discuss human infant cry with respect to the vocalizations of non-human primates.

## METHOD

Cries were recorded from 20 newborn infants from birth to the

---

[1]  University of Connecticut, Storrs, and Haskins Laboratories, New York City.
[2]  City University of New York, and Haskins Laboratories.
[3]  Harvard Medical School, Boston, Massachusetts.
[4]  Temple University, Philadelphia, Pennsylvania and Haskins Laboratories.

fourth day of life. An Ampex type 601 tape recorder was used with an Electro-Voice 633A microphone. The recordings were made in the hospital delivery room and in a room adjoining the hospital nursery. The tape recordings were edited and spectrograms were made using a Kay Electric Sound Spectrograph and a Voiceprint Sound Spectrograph. The sample analyzed included birth cries, 'fussing cries', 'angry cries', 'gurgles', 'hunger cries', 'shrieks', and inspiratory 'whistles'. The descriptive terms for these cries are consistent with clinical observations and impressions formed through an extensive study of infant behavior by one of the authors (P.W.). Most of the cries were spontaneous, some were elicited by pinches. The vocalizations encompassed the range that is normally produced by infants in good health.

## RESULTS

In Fig. 12 a spectrogram of a cry that was produced during the first five minutes of life by a male infant is presented. The bandwidth of the spectrograph's analyzing filter was 300 Hz. The fundamental frequency of phonation was about 400 Hz. The glottal excitation apparently was breathy since the effects of noise excitation are evident in the spectrogram. The noisy excitation indeed made it pos-

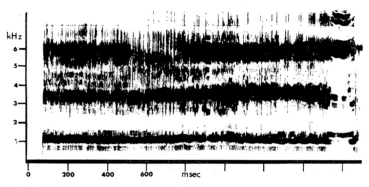

Fig. 12. Spectrogram of cry produced during first five minutes of life. The fundamental frequency is about 400 Hz. Note the formant frequencies at 1.1, 3.3 and 5.8 kHz.

sible to clearly resolve the energy concentrations that appear at approximately 1.1, 3.3 and 5.8 kHz. These energy concentrations must mirror the transfer function of the supralaryngeal vocal tract since they are spaced farther apart than the harmonics of the laryngeal excitation and at inharmonic intervals. These energy concentrations may not exactly specify the formant frequencies since harmonics of the laryngeal excitation are spaced at almost 400 Hz intervals. However, taking this uncertainty into account, we can approximate the formant frequencies and thereby infer the configuration of the infant's supralaryngeal vocal tract for this vocalization by making use of the acoustic theory of speech production (Chiba and Kajiyama, [1958]; Fant, [1960]).

The acoustic theory of speech production allows us to infer that the supralaryngeal vocal tract configuration of this infant approximated a 7.5 cm long uniform tube open at one end. The formants of a 7.5 cm long tube open at one end will occur at 1.1, 3.3, and 5.5 kHz since it will have resonances at intervals of:

$$(1) \quad \frac{(2k+1)\,C}{4L}$$

where $C$ = velocity of sound
$L$ = length of tube
$k$ is an integer $\geqq 0$

There is a surprising scarcity of information on the expected length of the neonatal vocal tract. Our estimate of 7.5 cm for the length of the infant's supralaryngeal vocal tract is consistent with comparative studies. Hopkin (1967), for example, notes that the neonatal tongue is approximately half the length of the adult tongue. Since the neonatal larynx is positioned higher in the vocal tract for a neonate than is the case for an adult (Noback [1923]) this estimate of 7.5 cm which is slightly less than half the length of the adult vocal tracts measured by Chiba and Kajiyama (1958) and Fant (1960) is quite reasonable.

In Fig. 13 another cry recorded at the birth of this same infant is presented. The analyzing filter's bandwidth was 300 Hz. Note that this cry consists of a short vocalization followed by a longer vocalization. The infant produced a short 'gurgle' followed by a cry. Energy concentrations are again apparent at 1, 3, and 5 kHz. for both

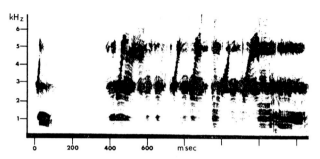

Fig. 13. Spectrogram of infant cry. Note the formants at 1, 3 and 5 KHz. These energy concentrations again reflect a supralaryngeal vocal tract configuration that approximates a uniform cross-section tube terminated at one end.

episodes of vocalization while harmonics of the laryngeal excitation are apparent at intervals of approximately 400 Hz. We can again infer that the supralaryngeal vocal tract configuration of this infant approximated the schwa vowel (i.e., a uniform cross-section tube) since the formants again occur at odd integral multiples.

Close examination of the set of spectrograms of the cries of the twenty neonates revealed no formant patterns that were not consistent with a supralaryngeal vocal tract configuration that approximated either a uniform cross-section or a slightly flared tube. In some instances the formants all moved higher or lower in frequency during the course of the cry. However, the intervals between the formants showed that the supralaryngeal vocal tract still approximated a tube (Lieberman [1968]). These formant transitions thus reflected changes in the overall length of the infants' supralaryngeal vocal tracts. Cineradiographic studies (Truby, Bosma and Lind [1965]) show that changes in the overall length of the neonatal supralaryngeal vocal tract occur during cries and are the result of laryngeal movements.

The formant pattern of the neonatal cries had energy present at intervals of $1F_c$, $3F_c$, and $5F_c$ (where $F_c$ = the first formant's center frequency) in approximately 80 percent of the cases. In the remaining 20 percent, energy instead was present at intervals of $F_o$, $2F_o$, $3F_o$, etc., where $F_o = 2F_c$. Under these conditions the neonates' supralaryngeal vocal tracts apparently resembled a uniform tube open at both ends. It was not possible to correlate this pattern with the descriptive terms that were used to characterize the cries except that it did not occur during any of the cries that were labelled 'fussing'. In Fig. 14 an example of this formant pattern is presented.

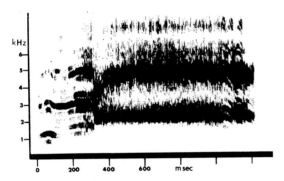

Fig. 14. Example of cry that starts with periodic excitation shifting to aperiodic excitation. Note initial formants at 1.25, 3.0 and 5.0 kHz. Energy concentrations then shift to 2.25 and 4.8 kHz. with aperiodic excitation. The supralaryngeal vocal tract configuration apparently approximates a tube with uniform boundary conditions when the glottal opening is large during the aperiodic breathy excitation.

This cry was produced seven minutes after birth by the same infant of Fig. 12 and 13. The analyzing filter's bandwidth was again 300 Hz. Note the presence of harmonics of the laryngeal excitation at the start of this utterance. Energy concentrations are present during the initial, voiced part of the utterance at 1.25, 3.0 and 5.0 kHz. Note that the cry loses its harmonic structure after 300 msec. where it becomes noisy. Note the abrupt discontinuity in the first energy concentration which shifts to 2.25 kHz. The second energy concentration occurs at 4.8 kHz. during this noisy part of the cry. The supralaryngeal vocal tract seems to be resonating as a half wave rather than as a quarter wave oscillator. The higher formants are multiples of the first formant which now occurs at twice the frequency of the first formant of the quarter wave resonator. The resonances of a uniform tube open at both ends will occur at intervals of:

$$(2) \quad \frac{(k)\,C}{2L} \qquad \begin{array}{l} \text{where } C = \text{the velocity of sound} \\ \qquad L = \text{the length of the tube,} \\ \qquad k \text{ is an integer} \geq 1 \end{array}$$

The first formant of a supralaryngeal vocal tract that resembles a uniform tube will therefore abruptly double in frequency when the boundary condition at the larynx changes from a closed state to an open state. The formants of a uniform tube open at both ends will also occur at regular intervals. The boundary condition at the infant's larynx therefore approximated an open termination when the laryngeal excitation changed to aperoidic noise at 300 msec. The most likely explanation for the change in the laryngeal excitation's character at 300 msec. is that the infant fails to increase the medial compression of his vocal cords as he increases his subglottal air pressure. He would thus blow his vocal cords apart preventing phonation and producing noiselike aperiodic excitation of his supralarungeal vocal tract which would be terminated by the open glottis.

Truby, Bosma and Lind (1965) in their study of neonatal vocalizations present spectrograms that show similar effects. They also present simultaneous plots of esophageal air pressure which indicate that these effects occur when the subglottal air pressure exceeds a critical level (about 6 cm $H_2O$ above the mean subglottal pressure). The infant's vocal cords are then thrown into an open position because he apparently does not modify the medial compression of his larynx (Van den Berg [1960]) during the cry.

Note that the laryngeal excitation becomes periodic at the end of the utterance in Fig. 14 (after 1000 msec.) where subglottal air pressure typically falls at the end of the unmarked breath-group (Lieberman [1967]). The fundamental frequency also abruptly falls during the last 100 msec. of the breath-group since the fundamental frequency of phonation is a function of both laryngeal muscular maneuvers and the transglottal air pressure drop.

It seems reasonable to attribute the changes in formant pattern and laryngeal excitation associated with the utterance in Fig. 14 to a state of minimum control, or indeed of noncontrol by the infant. The infant does not adjust his larynx so that phonation can continue as the subglottal air pressure rises. Perhaps the infant larynx is inherently incapable of withstanding high subglottal air pressures. However, whether the problem is a matter of laryngeal control or of laryngeal development the changes in formant pattern are concomitant with the change in laryngeal source characteristics from periodic excitation (which involves an adducted state of the larynx) to aperiodic noise which involves an open glottis. Truby, Bosma and Lind (1965) attribute similar changes in spectrographic displays to a special mode of phonation which they term 'hyperphonation'. We instead believe that these energy concentrations at widely spaced regular intervals reflect the formants of a supralaryngeal vocal tract shape that resembles a uniform tube that has similar, open boundary conditions at each end. Similar effects also appear to occur during the vocalizations of nonhuman primates.

Other phenomena also differentiate neonatal cry from adult speech. We found that the fundamental frequency of phonation, in general, was not stable during neonatal cry. In Fig. 15 a spectrogram is presented of a cry that was in response to pain stimulation from the infant shown in Fig. 14, 35 minutes after birth. The bandwidth of the analyzing filter was 150 Hz. The narrower bandwidth

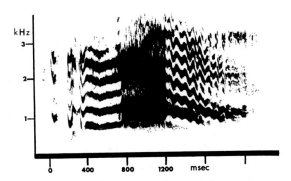

Fig. 15. Spectrogram showing large periodic variations in fundamental frequency that occur at a rate of approximately 12 Hz. The effective bandwidth of the spectrograph's analyzing filter was 150 Hz.

was achieved by playing the tape recording back at twice its normal speed. The time scale of the spectrogram is thus compressed while the frequency scale of the spectrogram is expanded. Individual harmonics of the laryngeal excitation are clearly resolved except for the middle portion of the utterance where some turbulent noiselike energy also occurs. Note the large periodic variations in fundamental frequency that occur at a rate of approximately 12 Hz. Variations in fundamental frequency like these frequently occur during the vocalizations of newborn infants.

### Correlations with Previous Studies of Infant Cry

The cineradiographic data reported by Truby, Bosma and Lind (1965) confirm that the supralaryngeal vocal tract configuration for newborn infant cry is almost rigid. They note that:

Direct inspection and radiographic observation reveal that the oral structures move little. The mandible is held tensely in open position, perhaps opening during cry and closing slightly during inspirations. The tongue tip becomes separated from its suckling or resting apposition to the lips and to oral surface of palate and maxillary alveolar ridge, and the tongue tip protrudes ventrad and cephalad from the tongue body. On inspection, the anterior portion of the tongue is seen to be tensed in concave contour . . . the mouth may be essentially immobilized in position. (p. 70)

The only movements that appear to occur during neonatal cry involve gross laryngeal maneuvers where the larynx moved upwards and downwards. Similar laryngeal maneuvers also occur during ape and monkey cries (Lieberman [1968]). The cineradiographic photographs reproduced by Bosma, Truby and Lind furthermore showed that the velum was either open or closed throughout each utterance. The earliest vocalizations appeared to be nasalized while some of the latter vocalizations appeared to be made while the velum was closed.

Lynip (1951), in a study of infant vocalizations, made spectrograms of utterances produced by one girl from birth to 60 weeks. He concluded that the '. . . infant's pre-speech utterances are essentially incomparable to adult sounds'. (p. 246). His conclusion is correct insofar as very young children produce schwa-like utterances where all the formants are transposed to higher frequencies than those typical of adult vocalizations. Winitz (1960) in a study of infants whose ages ranged from 9-15 months (mean age 11.5 months) found that they indeed produced the entire range of human vowels. The disagreement between Lynip's and Winitz's conclusions appears to reflect Lynip's paying most attention to utterances recorded between birth and one month of life while Winitz concentrates on much older infants. Our results are consistent with Lynip's data for cries recorded between birth and two to three months of life for his subject.

One of the oft repeated statements about language acquisition is that children, when they babble, produce the sounds of all languages known to man (Miller [1951]). Our data indicate that infants certainly do not start with this capability from birth onwards. Perceptually-based studies of the utterances of infants tend to support our conclusions. Irwin (1948), for example, reports that infants do not use any back vowels during the first three months of life. He notes that 25 percent of their vocalizations are transcribed as /I/, 45 % as /E/ and 25 % as /V/. In all likelihood Irwin's observers categorized some of the infant schwalike sounds as /I/ or /E/ because the short length of the infant vocal tract produces higher formant frequencies than is the case for adult speech.

## CONCLUDING DISCUSSION

Newborn human infants, like non-human primates, do not execute any maneuvers of their supralaryngeal vocal tracts during vocalizations except for gross laryngeal maneuvers. The shape of their supralaryngeal vocal tract appears to approximate a uniform cross-section, schwa-like, configuration.

Human infants appear to start life equipped with a vocal tract that differs from that of the adult vocal tract in configuration as well as in size. Indeed, the vocal tract of the newborn in some ways is more similar to the vocal tract of a non-human primate than it is to the adult human vocal tract. The position of the larynx in the human neonate is quite high. The epiglottis is at the level of the first cervical vertebra while the inferior border of the cricoid is at the level of the fourth cervical vertebra (Noback [1928]). These positions are similar in Gorilla (Negus, [1949]). In an adult, these cartilages are respectively at the level of the third and sixth cervical vertebrae. The thyroid cartilage of the neonate lies contiguous to the hyoid bone (Eckenhoff, [1951]) placing the epiglottis in fairly close proximity to the velum and keeping the root of the tongue within the oral cavity. Furthermore, the infant tongue is large, much closer to its adult proportions, by comparison to the oral cavity. The mandible will undergo dramatic downward, forward growth, which when coupled with the downward growth of the upper alveolar process, and the upward growth of the lower alveolar process, and the descent of the root of the tongue in conjunction with the descent of the larynx, eventually encloses the tongue in an oral cavity such as it is known in the adult (Brodie [1949]). However, in the neonate, the short, broad tongue fills the entire mouth and in its resting state is superiorly in contact with the entire length of the palate, laterally with the buccinator and anteriorly with parts of the jaws so that the mouth is closed by the action of the lips (Scammon [1923]; Brodie [1950]). During suckle, a position is maintained between the tongue tip and the lower lip. Only during infant cry is the mouth wide open and the tongue separated from its apposition with the palate and lower lip (Bosma [1967]).

The upper pharynx also differs markedly in the neonate and as a result is much less mobile than in the adult. In the new-born, the upper pharynx is a narrow tube, the longest diameter of which runs anteroposteriorly rather than superoinferiorly as it does in the adult (Braislin [1940]). The roof of the infant's pharynx slopes gently downward from the chonae to the dorsal wall of the mesopharynx and therefore the epipharynx of the infant does not have a dorsal or posterior wall (Bosma and Fletcher [1962]). The newborn infant, like a nonhuman primate, thus lacks a pharyngeal region that can vary its cross-sectional area. In fully developed human speech, pharyngeal volume changes over a ten-to-one range as the root of the tongue, which forms the anterior pharyngeal wall, moves. These changes in pharyngeal volume are essential for producing phonetic contrasts, e.g., /a/ versus /i/ (Chiba and Kajiyama [1958]; Fant [1960]). Although some of the limitations of the vocal repertoire of human neonates may be due to deficiencies in the central control of the vocal apparatus, the newborn human infant like the non-human primates is restricted by the limitations of his vocal apparatus (Lieberman [1968]; Lieberman, Klatt and Wilson, [1969]).

Human infants, unlike monkeys and apes, eventually produce the full range of human speech. The question that confronts us now is, when and under what conditions do infants go beyond the non-human stage? Human infants start life with a speech production apparatus that in many ways resembles the non-human primate vocal apparatus. We know that the non-human primate vocal apparatus is inherently incapable of producing the range of human speech. Human evolution involved, among many other factors, the development of the peripheral structures involved in speech production. We need to study the development of cry and babble in human infants with respect to both the development of the output mechanism, i.e., the vocal tract, and the development of the central control of the vocal tract. We think that the answers to these questions as well as the overall sequence that is involved in the infant's acquisition of the phonetic level of language will be relevant to the broader question of the nature of human linguistic ability.

## REFERENCES

Bosma, J. F.
   1967   "Human infant oral function", in *Symposium on Oral Sensation and Perception*, Chapter 40, edited by J. F. Bosma (Springfield, Illinois, Charles C. Thomas) 98-110.
Bosma, J. F., and S. G. Fletcher
   1961   "The upper pharynx, a review, Part I, Embryology and Anatomy", *Annals Otol. Rhinol. Laryngol.*, LXX, 935-973.
Braislin, W. C.
   1919   "A study of some casts of the infantile pharynx with special reference to the eustachian tubes", *Annals of Otol., Rhinol. and Laryngol.* IXX, 36-74.
Brodie, A. G.
   1949   "On the growth pattern of the human head from three months to eight years of life", *Am. J. Anat.*, LXVIII, 209-259.

1950 "Anatomy and physiology of the head and neck, musculature", *Am. J. Orth.*, XXVI, 831-837.

Chiba, T. and M. Kajiyama
1958 *The Vowel, Its Nature and Structure* (Tokyo, Phonetic Society of Japan).

Eckenhoff, J. E.
1951 "Some anatomic considerations of the infant larynx influencing endotracheal anesthesia", *Anesthesiology*, XII, 401-410.

Fant, C. G. M.
1960 *Acoustic Theory of Speech Production*, (The Hague, Mouton).

Hopkin, G. B.
1967 "Neonatal and adult tongue dimensions", *Angle Orthodontia*, 27, 132-133.

Irwin, O. C.
1948 "Infant speech: development of vowel sounds", *J. Speech and Hearing Disorders*, 13, 31-34.

Lieberman, P.
1963 "Some acoustic measures of the fundamental periodicity of normal and pathologic larynges", *J. Acoust. Soc. Am.*, 35, 344-353.
1967 *Intonation, Perception and Language* (Cambridge, Mass., M.I.T. Press).
1968 "Primate vocalizations and human linguistic ability", *J. Acoust. Soc. Am.*, 44, 1574-1584.

Lieberman, P., K. S. Harris and P. Wolff
1968 "Newborn infant cry in relation to nonhuman primate vocalizations", *J. Acoust. Soc. Am.*, 44, 365 (A).

Lieberman, P., D. L. Klatt and W. A. Wilson
1969 "Vocal tract limitations on the vowel repertoires of rhesus monkey and other nonhuman primates", *Science*, 164, 1185-1187.

Lynip, A. W.
1951 "The uses of magnetic devices in the collection and analysis of the preverbal utterances of an infant", *Genetic Psychol. Monog.* 44, 221-262.

Miller, G. A.
1951 *Language and Communication* (New York, McGraw-Hill).

Negus, V. E.
1949 *The Comparative Anatomy and Physiology of the Larynx* (New York, Hafner Publishing Co.).

Noback, G. J.
1923 "The developmental topography of the larynx, trachea, and lungs in fetus, new-born, infant and child", *Am. J. Dis. Child.* XXVI, 515-533.

Scammon, R.
1923 "A summary of the anatomy of the infant and child", in *Pediatrics*, Vol. I, Chapter III, edited by Isaac Apt (Philadelphia, W. B. Saunders) 296-297.

Truby, H. M., J. F. Bosma and F. Lind
1965 *Newborn Infant Cry* (Uppsala, Almqvist and Wiksells).

Van den Berg, J.
1960 Vocal ligaments versus registers, *Current Problems in Phoniatrics and*

*Logopedics*, 1, 19-34.

Winitz, H.
1960 "Spectrographic investigation of infant vowels", *J. Genetic Psychol.*, 96, 171-181.

# VOCAL TRACT LIMITATIONS ON THE VOWEL REPERTOIRES OF RHESUS MONKEY AND OTHER NONHUMAN PRIMATES

PHILIP LIEBERMAN, DENNIS H. KLATT*, WILLIAM A. WILSON**

## ABSTRACT

The vowel repertoire of a rhesus monkey (Macaca mulatta) was explored by means of a computer program that calculated formant frequencies from the area function of the animal's supralaryngeal vocal tract, which was systematically varied within the limits imposed by anatomical constraints. The resulting vowels were compared with those of humans and with recorded vocalizations of nonhuman primates. The computer model indicates that the acoustic 'vowel space' of a rhesus monkey is quite restricted compared to that of the human. This limitation results from the lack of a pharyngeal region that can change its cross-sectional area. These animals thus lack the output mechanism necessary for production of human speech. Man's speech output mechanism is apparently species-specific.

Vocalizations of captive rhesus monkey, chimpanzee, and gorilla have been recorded and analyzed by means of sound spectrograms and oscillograms.[1] The acoustic analysis suggested that these animals lack the ability to produce the articulatory maneuvers necessary to produce the full range of human speech. The general assumption that the vocal mechanisms of these animals are sufficiently well developed to permit the articulation of words[2] would thus be wrong.

Human speech is essentially the product of a source (the larynx for vowels) and a supralaryngeal vocal-tract transfer function. The

\* Department of Electrical Engineering, Massachusetts Institute of Technology, Cambridge.
\*\* Department of Psychology, University of Connecticut.

[1] P. Lieberman, *J. Acoust. Soc. Amer.* (1968) 44, 1575.
[2] W. N. Kellogg, *Science* (1968) 162, 423.

supralaryngeal vocal tract, in effect, filters the source.[3] The activity of the larynx determines the fundamental frequency of the vowel, whereas its formant frequencies are the resonant modes of the supra-laryngeal vocal-tract transfer function. The formant frequencies are determined by the area function of the supralaryngeal tract.[3] The vowels /a/ and /i/, for example, have different formant frequencies though they may have the same fundamental frequency. The object of this study is to extend the acoustic analysis[1] that indicated that the nonhuman primates' vocalizations are restricted to schwa-like cries produced by means of a supralaryngeal vocal tract with a cross section that is uniform along its length. (An example of the schwa is the first vowel in the word *about.*) Our acoustic analysis was per-force limited to the sounds that animals actually uttered. Our present method makes use of a computer-implemented model of the supralaryngeal vocal tract of a rhesus monkey (*Macaca mulatta*) that we systematically manipulated. We thus were able to explore the full range of vowels that a rhesus monkey could produce if he exploited all the degrees of freedom of his supralaryngeal vocal tract Our analysis of the possible range of monkey vocalizations thus can be independent of the restrictions inherent in the analysis of a limit-ed set of actual utterances. There is, of course, no guarantee that a monkey will in fact use all of the articulatory maneuvers that we simulate. Itani[4], for example, reports that wild Japanese monkeys seldom use their lips during cries, though they are physically able to move their lips. However, we can explore the inherent limits of the output device.

A plaster casting was made of the oral cavity of a monkey soon after it died. The monkey's tongue and lips were positioned in an approximation of an aggressive 'bark'[5]. The plaster casting was then sectioned at intervals of 0.5 cm and the cross-sectional areas were determined by weighing paper tracings of the sections on an analytical balance. This area is presented as the solid line in Fig. 16.

[3]  T. Chiba and M. Kajiyama, *The Vowel, Its Nature and Structure* (Tokyo, Phonetic Society of Japan, 1958); G. Fant, *Acoustic Theory of Speech Production* (The Hague, Mouton, 1960).
[4]  J. Itani, *Primates* (1963) 4, 11.
[5]  T. E. Rowell and R. A. Hinde, *Proc. Zool. Soc. London* (1962) 138, 279.

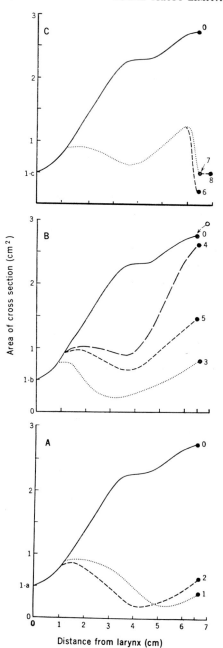

Fig. 16. Area functions of supralaryngeal vocal tract modeled by computer and corresponding vowel formant frequencies. Curve 0 is the unperturbed vocal tract of the rhesus monkey. The first formant frequency of this area function, $F_1$, is 1503 hz, $F_2$ is 4007 hz and $F_3$ is 6287 hz. (a) Curves 1 and 2 are perturbed area functions analogous to human high, front vowels, and their formant frequencies, respectively, are 867, 4533 and 6816 hz and 971, 4475 and 6526 hz. (b) Curves 3, 4 and 5 are perturbed area functions analogous to human low, back vowels. Their respective formant frequencies are: 1144, 3867 and 6817 hz; 1542, 3816 and 6415 hz; 1354, 3918 and 6461 hz. (c) Curves 6, 7 and 8 are perturbed area functions analogous to human rounded, back vowels. Their corresponding formant frequencies are, respectively: 1010, 3103 and 6175 hz; 1212, 3465 and 6881 hz; and 1034, 3152 and 6093 hz.

The acoustic waveform corresponding to a vowel can be regarded as the output of a vocal-tract filter system which is excited by vibrations of the vocal cord. It is the transfer function of the vocal tract that determines the vowel uttered because the volume velocity waveform at the vocal cords (the source) and the radiation impedance at the lips (the load) are relatively constant during vowel production and independent of the particular vowel.

The (frequency domain) transfer function of the vocal tract is determined by an area function which gives the cross-sectional area of the vocal tract as a function of position along the tract. For frequencies of interest, the vocal tract behaves as a linear system satisfying the one-dimensional wave equation.[6] A closed-form solution to the wave equation for arbitrary area functions is not known; so it is necessary to use an algorithm to find an approximate solution for individual sample area functions.

The algorithm used in the computer program represents the vocal tract by a series of contiguous cylindrical sections, each of fixed area.[7] Each section can be described by a characteristic impedance and a complex propagation constant, both being well-known quantities for uniform cylindrical tubes. Junctions between individual sections satisfy the constraints of continuity of pressure and conservation of volume velocity. The transfer function (magnitude and phase) is calculated directly as a function of frequency. Natural frequencies (formants) are determined from the phase spectrum.

In this fashion the computer program calculated the three lowest formant frequencies. (The lowest resonances are the perceptually most important aspects of a vocalization produced with a given supralaryngeal vocal tract configuration.) These formant frequencies are presented in Fig. 16.

We then systematically explored the possible range of supralaryngeal vocal-tract area functions that a rhesus monkey could make by moving his tongue, lips and jaw. The computer program was used

[6]   L. L. Beranek, *Acoustics* (New York, McGraw-Hill, 1954).
[7]   W. L. Henke, "Dynamic articulatory model of speech production using computer simulation", thesis, Massachusetts Institute of Technology (1966), appendix B.

to determine the formant frequencies of the first three formants for each configuration. We estimated the range of articulatory maneuvers by manipulating the supralaryngeal vocal tract of an anesthetized monkey and by taking into consideration the continuity constraints imposed by the monkey's tongue as well as the effects of different jaw angles and lip rounding. In doubtful cases we allowed greater deviations from the 'unperturbed' area function derived from the casting.

In Fig. 16a the dashed lines represent vocal tract configurations (for two different degrees of tongue height) that would be most likely to lead to the production of an unrounded high vowel. These result from changes in the tract toward that shape of a human vocal tract that is characteristic of the production of /i/. We note that $F_1$ decreases relative to the unperturbed vocal tract whereas $F_2$ increases. In Fig. 1b the three dashed lines represent vocal tract configurations analogous to low back vowels—that is, vowels produced with a tongue constriction toward the back of the mouth while the jaw is open or low, for example /a/. In Fig. 16c the dashed lines represent configurations for rounded back vowels—that is, vowels in which the lips are rounded, such as /u/. In configuration 8 we have tried to account for the lengthening of the vocal tract that can occur with lip rounding, as, for example, in the human vowel /u/.

The ratio of the maximum constrictions for these vocal tract configurations relative to the dimensions of the unperturbed vocal tract is similar to that measured by Fant[3] for human vowels. We have plotted the calculated first and second formant frequencies that correspond to our unperturbed and perturbed monkey vocal tract configurations in Fig. 17. We have also plotted the formant frequencies measured by Fant for a male human speaker for the vowels /a/, /u/ and /i/. These three vowels delimit the human 'vowel space'. The length of this speaker's supralaryngeal vocal tract was 17 cm for /a/. We have therefore multiplied the formant frequencies measured by Fant by the ratio 2.6 to take account of the fact that the tract length of the monkey is 6.5 cm, but that of the adult human who was measured by Fant was 17 cm. This procedure is valid for $F_1$ and $F_2$ of /a/ and $F_2$ of /u/ and /i/ where the behavior of the vocal

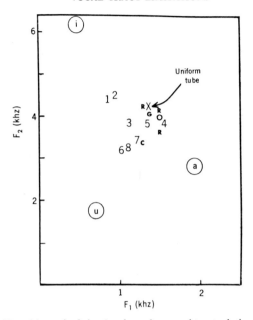

Fig. 17. Vowel 'space' of simulated monkey vocal tract relative to human vowel space and natural ape and monkey cries (1). Chimpanzee cry noted by letter C, Gorilla by G and rhesus monkey by R. The formant frequencies that would correspond to a uniform tube, 6.5 cm in length, terminated at one end are also plotted. All of the formant frequencies have been scaled toward those of the rhesus monkey to compensate for differences in overall vocal tract length.

tract can, as a first approximation, be represented by means of two or three tube models.[3,8]

We have also plotted the previously analyzed formant frequencies of both ape and monkey cries that were produced with the vocal tract terminated by a high laryngeal impedance.[1,9] We have also

[8] K. N. Stevens, in *Human Communication, A Unified View*, E. E. David, Jr., and P. B. Denes, Eds. (New York, McGraw-Hill, 1969).

[9] Some of the ape and monkey cries were apparently produced while the animals' larynges were open wide[1]. These cries are not plotted in Fig. 17 because the vocal-tract boundary conditions do not correspond to the computer model. However the acoustic analysis indicated that the shape of the animals' supralaryngeal vocal tract when they produced these cries still appeared to approximate a uniform tube. These cries therefore would not change our conclusions concerning the range of supralaryngeal vocal tract configurations that underlie these animals' vocalizations.

scaled up these formant frequencies to take account of the longer vocal tracts of these animals relative to rhesus monkey. The formant frequencies that would correspond to a uniform tube, 6.5 cm long, terminated at one end are also plotted in Fig. 17. The actual monkey and ape cries occupy only part of the vowel space of our computer-generated vowels. The only natural cry that is a signficant deviation from this schwa vowel is the chimpanzee cry which was produced by the animal with its lips rounded[1]; the formant frequencies of this cry correspond most closely to configuration 7 of Fig. 16c, which represents the least rounded of our simulated rounded back vowels. Our computer-modeled configurations of the perturbed monkey vocal tract thus encompass and extend beyond the 'acoustic vowel space' that was measured for actual utterances of nonhuman primates. The nonhuman primates previously recorded did not, in fact, use all of the articulatory maneuvers that we simulated for the rhesus monkey by means of the computer model.

The computer model further indicates that the possible acoustic vowel space of a monkey is quite restricted compared to the human range. Even if a rhesus monkey were able to manipulate his supralaryngeal vocal tract to make use of all of the possibilities that we considered in our computer model, he would not be able to produce the full range of human vowels. We can thus conclude that the vocal apparatus of the rhesus monkey is inherently incapable of producing the range of human speech.

In Fig. 18 we have presented schematized area functions for the human vowels /a/, /u/ and /i/ where we have approximated the vocal tract by means of uniform tubes for illustrative purposes. We have based these approximations on Fant's data[3]. The supralaryngeal vocal tract can essentially be divided into an anterior and a posterior cavity. The cross-sectional area of the pharyngeal region in man can be constricted while the front of the mouth is open as in /a/. A large cross-sectional area can also be produced in the pharyngeal region with either a constricted anterior passage as in /i/ or a large cavity as in /u/. The nonhuman primates cannot produce vocal-tract area functions like man's because both the apes and

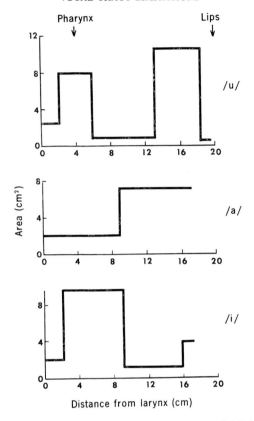

Fig. 18. Schematized area functions for the human vowels /a/, /u/ and /i/. Note that the area of the pharyngeal region is independent of the area of the front part of the supralaryngeal vocal tract.

monkeys lack a pharyngeal region like man's,[1, 10] where the body of the tongue forms a movable anterior wall. We have reproduced an illustration (Fig. 10) from Negus[11], indicating relative positions

[10]  V. E. Negus, *The Comparative Anatomy and Physiology of the Larynx* (New York, Hafner, 1949).

[11]  We thank Professor W. Henke for providing the computer program to calculate formant frequencies from area functions. Supported in part by PHS grants DE 01774, HD 01994, NB 04332-06, and MH 10972. The computation facilities were provided by project MAC, a Massachusetts Institute of Technology program sponsored by ARPA under contract with ONR.

of the palate and larynx in the nonhuman primates and in man. The nonhuman primates lack a pharyngeal region like man's, where the cross-sectional area continually changes during speech. The inability of apes to mimic human speech[2] is thus an inherent limitation of their vocal mechanisms. Some of man's recent ancestors also may have been unable to produce the full range of human speech; the skeletal evidence of human evolution shows a series of changes from the primate vocal tract that may have been, in part, necessary for the generation of speech[1]. The human speech-output mechanism thus should be viewed as part of man's species-specific linguistic endowment.

# ON THE ACOUSTIC ANALYSIS OF PRIMATE VOCALIZATIONS

PHILIP LIEBERMAN

### Abstract

The acoustic theory of speech production relates articulatory maneuvers to acoustic attributes of speech. Some procedures are discussed that make use of this theory to analyze the vocalizations of nonhuman primates. These procedures make use of sound spectrograms, oscillograms and computer-implemented analogs of the primate vocal apparatus as well as anatomical measurements. The use of these techniques in recent studies of nonhuman primate vocalizations is reviewed. These studies show that nonhuman primates lack the anatomical apparatus that is necessary for the production of the full range of human speech. Some unresolved questions concerning the structure of nonhuman primate utterances are discussed with regard to human linguistic ability.

The object of this paper is to review some of the analytical methods that are appropriate for the study of the phonetics of primate utterances. We shall discuss the acoustic theory of speech production and some of the known differences between the nonhuman primates and man. We shall also discuss some possible similarities in the acoustic communications of man and the nonhuman primates that should be studied in more detail.

Although research on the acoustic and articulatory bases of speech communication has a long history, in the past 30 years a quantitative acoustic theory of speech production has been developed (Chiba & Kajiyama [1958]; Fant [1960]). This theory allows us to relate the acoustic speech signal to the articulatory maneuvers that humans use when they speak. The acoustic theory of speech production also permits us to evaluate the acoustic significance of articulatory maneuvers and anatomical structures.

## PROCEDURES INVOLVED IN ACOUSTIC ANALYSIS

We will use the term 'acoustic analysis' in a rather loose sense since we will actually describe some of the techniques that have been used in two recent studies (Lieberman [1968]; Lieberman, Klatt & Wilson [1969]). These studies used anatomical- and computer-modeling procedures to investigate the vocal repertoires of nonhuman primates.

Obviously, one must have adequate tape recording facilities in order to analyze the utterances of any animals. We used Sony Type TC 800 tape recorders with both Sony Type F85 and General Radio Type 1560 P5 microphones at a tape speed of 7.5 in/sec; the response was 6 dB down at 16 kHz. The system was flat to 12 kHz. The tape recorder and microphone power supplies were battery-powered, which made recordings in zoos practical. The acoustical analysis involved the use of a sound spectrograph (Voiceprint), an oscilloscope (Honeywell Visicorder), and a medium-size digital computer (Digital Equipment Corporation PDP-9).

The upper limit on the frequency response of our recording system appeared to be adequate for the primate vocalizations recorded in these studies. If one were interested in the smaller primates, e.g., squirrel monkeys (*Saimiri sciureus*) whose vocalizations appear to involve higher frequency components, the upper limit on the frequency response of the recording system would have to be higher.

## ACOUSTIC THEORY OF SPEECH PRODUCTION

It is both convenient and correct to regard human speech in terms of two quantities: an excitation source and a filter. In the production of the vowel /a/, for example, the quasiperiodic opening and closing motions of the vocal cords generate a periodic excitation source. This laryngeal source is filtered by the supralaryngeal vocal tract. The area function of the supralaryngeal vocal tract determines the filter function of the supralaryngeal vocal tract. The local energy maxima of the supralaryngeal filter function are the 'formant' frequencies. The vowel /a/ for an adult male might have formant frequencies of 700, 900 and 2700 Hz. The formants for /i/ for the same speaker might be 300, 2100 and 3200 Hz (Fant [1960]). The speaker could produce either vowel using the same laryngeal excitation. He could, for example, phonate at a fundamental frequency of 130 Hz for both /i/ and /a/. The area function of his supralaryngeal vocal tract would, however, be quite different for these two vowels. The speaker could alternatively phonate the two vowels at different fundamental frequencies, say 130 and 200 Hz. His vocal cords would open and close at different rates in order to produce these two different fundamental frequencies. The phonetic quality of the vowels /a/ and /i/ would, however, be preserved. The speaker could even whisper the two vowels by keeping his vocal cords in an open position and exciting the supralaryngeal vocal tract by means of a turbulent noiselike source. The formants for /a/ and /i/ in all these cases would be a function of the area function of the supralaryngeal vocal tract.

## MEASUREMENTS OF NONHUMAN PRIMATE VOCALIZATIONS

Figure 1 shows a reproduced spectrogram from one of the studies of primate vocalizations that we will discuss (Lieberman[1968]). This vocalization was produced by a 3-year-old female gorilla at a moderate level of intensity when food was withheld. The spectrogram was made using the 'normal' display function on the Voiceprint machine that produces a 'conventional' sound spectrogram. Two display options are available on the machine: 'normal' and 'contour'. In both displays energy is displayed as a function of frequency vs. time. In the 'normal' mode the intensity of energy at a particular frequency is a function of the degree of blackness of the display. In the 'contour' display intensity is quantized at 6 dB gradients and a display that resembles a contour map results. We generally preferred to use the 'normal' display (the contour display seems to show too much information for visual interpretation). The bandwidth of the spectrograph's analyzing filter was set to 300 Hz, and the frequency preemphasis circuits were set at the 'Flat' position, since there is more high-frequency energy in the glottal excitation of the gorilla than is the case for human vocalization. This is also the case for rhesus monkey and chimpanzee vocalizations.

The fundamental frequency of phonation, which can be measured from the vertical striations that appear in the wide-band spectrogram, was unstable and ranged from 100 to 120 Hz. Large pitch perturbations, i.e. rapid fluctuations in the glottal periodicity, occurred from one period to the next. The laryngeal output of the gorilla appears to be very noisy and turbulent. Energy concentration can be noted in Fig. 1 at 500, 1500, and 2400 Hz. Measurements of the skull and mandible of an adult gorilla yield an estimated supralaryngeal vocal tract length of 18 cm. If a gorilla uttered the schwa vowel (the first vowel in the word *about*), that is, a vowel having a vocal tract shape that approximates a uniform tube open at one end, we would expect to find formant frequencies at 460, 1400, and 2300 Hz since the resonances of a uniform tube open at one end will occur at intervals of:

$$\frac{(2k + 1) (C)}{4L}$$

where $C$ = velocity of sound, $L$ = length of the tube, and $k$ is an integer $\geq 0$. We can, therefore, infer that the energy concentrations in this spectrogram reflect the transfer function of the gorilla's supralaryngeal vocal tract in the schwa position. Note that these energy concentrations are not spaced at harmonic multiples of the fundamental frequency.

The main characteristic of this utterance is that the output of the gorilla's larynx is being modified by the resonances of the supralaryngeal vocal tract as is the case for human speech. Note that this is in sharp contrast to the calls of birds, where the fundamental frequency and harmonics of the syrinx's output completely characterize the acoustic nature of the cry (Thorpe [1961]; Greenewalt [1968]).

Note that the bandwidth of the spectrograph's analyzing filter was 300 Hz. Narrow bandwidth analysis would have made it quite difficult to determine the formant frequencies. Narrow bandwidth spectrograms are appropriate for the analysis of bird calls, where the acoustic characteristics of the signal are structured in terms of the fundamental frequency and harmonic structure of the excitation function (the output of the syrinx). They are insufficient, however, when the acoustic characteristics of the signal are determined in part by the transfer function of the supralaryngeal vocal tract's configuration, which acts as an acoustic filter on the excitation function.

The exclusive use of narrow bandwidth spectrograms can lead to descriptions that, although acoustically valid in terms of the narrow bandwidth analysis, are inappropriate in terms of the acoustically and perceptually significant aspects of the signal. Marler and Hamilton (1966), for example, note that ,"compared with the calls of birds, many sounds used by primates and other mammals are coarse, lacking the purity of tone and precise patterns of frequency modulation that occur in many passerine bird songs". This statement is true insofar as the primates do not produce cries that can be described in terms of one or two 'pure' sinusoidal components. Yet neither can human speech be described in terms of one or two pure tones, "...or precise patterns of frequency modulation...." If the methodology that is appropriate for the analysis of bird calls were used for the analysis of human speech it would be extremely difficult to isolate most of the significant phonologic elements. We would perhaps conclude that human speech employed 'coarse' sounds, i.e. sounds that were not inherently musical. The point here is, of course, that the acoustic analysis must be appropriate for the signal. In order to investigate the effects of the supralaryngeal vocal tract we must use analyzing filters that have a bandwidth sufficient to encompass two or more harmonics of the excitation function. This aspect of speech analysis is discussed in detail by Koenig, Dunn and Lacy (1946).

The sound spectrograph used in this study was manufactured by the Voiceprint Company of New Jersey. Other commercially available spectrographs such as those manufactured by the Kay Electric Company, Pine Brook, New Jersey, would also have been suitable. It is usually not necessary to use the 'contour displays' that are available on the Voiceprint machine. When detailed spectral information is necessary, 'sections' can be made with either the Voice-print or Kay Electric machines. It is, however, necessary to maintain adequate bandwidth in the spectrographic analysis if one wishes to determine formant frequencies.

In Fig. 5 a spectogram of one of the aggressive sounds of a rhesus monkey is presented (Lieberman [1968]). The cry was produced at a moderate degree of vocal effort while the monkey bared his teeth. Six normal monkeys were recorded over a period of 6 months in the monkey colony of the University of Connecticut at Storrs. This particular recording was made with the Sony Type F85 microphone. In Fig. 6 part of the oscillogram of this cry is shown. The first two 'bursts' are presented in the oscillogram, which was made as the tape recording was played back at one-fourth speed. The fundamental frequency of phonation is approximately 400 Hz. Note that the fundamental periodicity is very unstable at best. Parts of the waveform appear to be very turbulent. The waveform, in all, looks very much like those associated with pathologic human larynges where a hoarse vocal output results (Lieberman[1963]). The rhesus monkeys, like the gorillas and chimpanzees, are unable to produce sustained vocalizations that have a steady fundamental periodicity.

The spectrogram in Fig. 5 was also made from a tape that was played back at one-fourth speed. This procedure increased the effective bandwidth of the spectrograph by a factor of four. The effective bandwidth of the spectograph was thus 1200 Hz. Energy concentrations occurred at 1, 3 and 6 to 8 kHz. There was approximately 25 msec between each burst and glottal activity seems to have been sustained. Thus the cry is similar to a sequence of voiced stops in intervocalic position.

Unlike voiced stops in human speech, the closure of the vocal tract seems to have been effected by the animal's epiglottis and velum. The monkey's lips were retracted, exposing his teeth throughout the cry, so he could not have used his lips to obstruct his vocal tract. There are also no formant trasitions, which would occur of the supralaryngeal vocal tract were momentarily obstructed by the tongue. The larynx of a rhesus monkey is quite high in contrast to the position of the human vocal tract, and his epiglottis can seal his mouth off at the soft palate (Geist [1961]).

Note that the energy concentrations at 1, 3 and 6 to 8 kHz are again consistent with the resonances of a uniform tube open at one end. We anesthetized a 5-year-old male monkey and measured the length of his supralaryngeal vocal tract. With his lips rounded the length of the supralaryngeal vocal tract was 7.6 cm. The resonances of a uniform 7.6-cm-long tube open at one end are 1100, 3300 and 5500 Hz. We recorded a number of cries that the monkey made with his lips rounded at a low level of vocal effort. The recordings were made in a quiet room using the General Radio 1560-P5 microphone. The average values of $F_1$, $F_2$ and $F_3$ were 1300, 3000 and 4400 Hz, respectively. Thus the monkey was producing these cries with a slightly flared supralaryngeal vocal tract.

In Fig. 7 photographs of a casting of the oral cavity of a rhesus monkey are presented. The monkey's tongue and lips were positioned in an approximation of an aggressive 'bark,' (Rowell & Hinde [1962]), and a plaster-of-paris casting was made shortly after an experiment in which the monkey was sacrificed for other purposes. Note that the vocal tract of the monkey approximates a uniform cross section passage with a flared portion at the laryngeal end. Also note the shallowness of the pharyngeal 'bend' and the flatness of the monkey's tongue, which is apparent in the side view. The monkey's tongue fills up the shallow section delimited by the depth of the 'bend' at the laryngeal end of the oral cavity.

The nonhuman primates essentially lack a pharyngeal region like man's. In Fig. 9 a schematized view of the pharyngeal and oral regions of the human supralaryngeal vocal tract is presented. Note that the anterior wall of the pharyngeal region is formed by the back of the tongue. The human tongue is thick in comparison with its length. The shape of the pharyngeal region constantly changes during the production of human speech as the tongue moves backwards and forwards. The cross-sectional area of the pharynx varies, for example, over a ten-to-one range for the vowels /a/ and /i/ (Fant [1960]). The vowel /a/ is produced with a small pharyngeal cross-section while the /i/ is produced with a large cross-section. These variations in pharyngeal cross-sectional area are characteristic for consonants as well as vowels, and they are essential in the production of human speech.

In Fig 10 a semidiagrammatic representation of the nose, palate, tongue, pharynx, and larynx of a monkey, an ape, and man are reproduced from Negus (1949). Note the relative positions of the palate and larynx. The basis for the nonhuman primates' lack of tongue mobility appears to be anatomical. The pharyngeal region, which can vary its shape in man, has no real counterpart in these animals. Their larynges are positioned quite high compared to the human larynx, almost in line with the roof of the palate. And the tongues of these animals are thin compared to man's. The nonhuman primates do not have a pharynx where the root of a thick tongue forms a movable anterior wall. Zhinkin (1963), for example, in a cineradiographic study of baboon cries, shows that the baboon cannot vary the size of his pharynx. The tongues of the nonhuman primates are long and flat, and their supralaryngeal vocal tracts cannot assume the range of shape changes characteristic of human speech.

## COMPUTER-IMPLEMENTED ANALYSIS

The acoustic analysis of primate vocalizations discussed so far was perforce limited to the sounds that the animals actually uttered. We used our knowledge of the articulatory basis of human speech to infer that the limitations of these animals' vocal repertoires was anatomical. It is possible to see whether the limitation on the vowel repertoire of a nonhuman primate is actually due to the anatomical constraints imposed by his speech production apparatus (Lieberman, Klatt & Wilson [1969]). The method used employed a computer-implemented model of the supralaryngeal vocal tract of a rhesus monkey (*Macaca mulatta*) that was systematically manipulated.

The plaster casting of the oral cavity of a rhesus monkey pictured in Fig. 7 was sectioned at intervals of 0.5 cm and the cross-sectional area was determined by weighing paper tracings of the sections on an analytical balance. This area function is presented as the solid line in Fig. 16a.

As noted earlier, the acoustic theory of speech states that the acoustic waveform corresponding to a vowel can be regarded as the output of a vocal tract filter system that is excited by vocal cord vibrations. Temporal effects can be ignored when we differentiate sustained vowels. It is impossible to ignore temporal effects when we consider consonants like the stops /b,d,g/, etc., or diphthongs like /ai/.

The frequency domain transfer function of the vocal tract is determined by an area function that gives the cross-sectional area of the vocal tract as a function of position along the tract. For frequencies of interest, the vocal tract behaves as a linear solution satisfying the one-dimensional wave equation. A closed-form solution to the wave equation for arbitrary area functions is not known so it is necessary to use an algorithm to fiind an approximate solution for individual sample area functions.

The algorithm that has been used in the computer program (Henke [1966]) represents the vocal tract by a series of contiguous cylindrical sections, each of fixed area. Each section can be described by a characteristic impedance and a complex propagation constant, both of which are well-known quantities for uniform cylindrical tubes. Junctions between sections satisfy the constraints of continuity of pressure and conservation of volume velocity. The transfer function is calculated directly as a function of frequency. In this fashion the computer program calculated the three lowest formant frequencies. These formant frequencies are presented in Fig. 16a.

We systematically explored the possible range of supralaryngeal vocal tract area functions that a rhesus monkey could make by moving his tongue, lips, and jaw. The computer program was used to determine the formant frequencies for each configuration. In Fig. 16a the dashed lines represent vocal tract configurations for two different degrees of tongue height that would most likely lead to the production of an unrounded high vowel. These result from changes in the tract toward that shape of human vocal tract that is characteristic of the production of /i/. We also explored monkey vocal tract configurations that were perturbed in the direction of the human vowels /u/ and /a/. We estimated the range of articulatory maneuvers that are available to a monkey by manipulating the supralaryngeal vocal tract of an anesthetized monkey and by taking into consideration the continuity constraints imposed by the monkey's tongue as well as the effect of different jaw angles and lip rounding. In doubtful cases we allowed greater deviations from the 'unperturbed' area function derived from the casting. The computer program calculated the formant frequencies associated with each simulated monkey vocal tract configuration.

In Fig. 17 the first and second formant frequencies of these simulated vocal tract configurations are plotted together with the formant frequencies derived from actual nonhuman primate cries (Lieberman [1968]), and the vowels /a/, /u/ and /i/ measured by Fant (1960) for an adult male human speaker. These three vowels delimit the human 'vowel space'. We have scaled all the formant frequencies to the length of the rhesus monkey's vocal tract, which was 6.5 cm. Note that the actual monkey and ape cries noted by the letters C (chimpanzee), G (gorilla), and R (rhesus monkey) occupy only part of the vowel space of our computer-generated vowels. The nonhuman primates did not, in fact, use all of the articulatory maneuvers that we simulated for the rhesus monkey on the computer. Note that the computer model further indicates that the possible acoustic vowel space of a monkey is quite restricted compared to the human range. In other words, the vocal apparatus of the rhesus monkey is inherently incapable of producing the range of human speech. The results of the computer simulation (Lieberman, Klatt & Wilson [1969)] thus are consistent with the analysis of recorded nonhuman primate vocalizations (Lieberman [1968]).

## THE PHONETIC CODE, SOME UNANSWERED QUESTIONS

The experiments described herein merely set upper limits on the phonetic code that nonhuman primates might use in their vocal communications. They do not mean that the nonhuman primates are incapable of communication by means of cries. We have yet to 'decode' the communications of the nonhuman primates.

One of the primary characteristics of human language is that the relationship between sound and meaning is arbitrary in language. The difference between a system of cries, even though it may be highly developed, and a language is that the relationship between meaning and sound is fixed for cries. A high-pitched /a/, for example, might be the cry of pain for a particular species. It would always 'mean' pain no matter what sounds preceded or followed it. In contrast, the sound /a/ in a language may have no meaning in itself, nor might the sounds /m/ and /n/ in isolation. The sound sequence /man/ does have a particular semantic reference or meaning in English while the sound sequences /ma/ and /an/ have other meanings. The sequential coding of sounds in these examples is an essential aspect of linguistic systems.

Most work on animal communication has stressed the temporal ordering of sound sequences (Reynolds [1968]). Human speech is, of course, sequentially coded. But human speech is also a simultaneous code. We have independent control over a number of different 'phonologic features'. Each feature involves particular maneuvers of man's speech-producing apparatus, and each feature also has its acoustic 'correlates'. The phonologic features may, in effect, be viewed as matches between the constraints of man's speech-producing apparatus and auditory perception (Lieberman [1969]). The articulatory base of each feature is a maneuver that can readily be executed by man's speech-producing apparatus. The acoustic base of each feature is a signal that can be differentiated and categorized. We apparently 'code' and 'decode', that is, produce and perceive, speech in terms of these independent phonologic features (Liberman, Cooper, Shankweiler & Studdert-Kennedy [1967]).

Humans, for example, have independent control over the lips, larynx, and velum (the velum acts as a valve that can connect the nose to the mouth). We can, for example, close our lips or not, adduct our vocal cords or not, open our velum or not, etc. The difference between the sounds /b/ and /p/ in the words *bat* and *pat* is that the vocal cords are adducted when the lips are released in *bat* whereas they are open when the lips are released in *pat*. In a similar way *vat* differs from *mat* with respect to the state of the velum during the first part of the syllable.

We can, therefore, approach the acoustic communications of nonhuman species from at least two independent directions. We can explore the sequential coding of their cries. Birds, for example, do not appear to have control over a number of independent articulatory mechanisms. The time pattern of the fundamental frequency and harmonic content of the syrinx fully specify each bird call. It is therefore appropriate to concentrate on sequential coding in the analysis of these animals' communications systems. The nonhuman primates do not have the ability to produce the full range of human speech. They do, however, have the anatomical ability to control some phonologic features like voicing, nasality, and lip rounding. They have a much greater potential repertoire than do birds.

The question that should be answered is whether any of the nonhuman primates differentiate their meaningful cries by means of contrast in a simultaneous 'feature' code. If apes did communicate by means of cries that were differentiated by phonologic feature contrasts that were a subset of the phonologic features available to man, we would see a link between human language and nonhuman primate behavior. This question, of course, can be resolved only through research that couples acoustic analysis and behavioral techniques. The results should be of interest not only in furthering our knowledge of nonhuman primate behavior but of human linguistic ability and the development of human language.

## REFERENCES

Lieberman, P.
    1963    "Some acoustic measures of the fundamental periodicity of normal and pathologic larynges", *Journal of the Acoustical Society of America*, 35, 344-353.
    1968    "Primate vocalizations and human linguistic ability", *Journal of the Acoustic Society of America*, 44, 1574-1584.
    1969    "On the physical bases of phonologic features: *Language*," in *Status Report SR-15*, Haskins Laboratories, New York City.
Chiba, T. and M. Kajiyama
    1958    *The vowel, its nature and structure* (Tokyo, Phonetic Society of Japan).
Fant, C. G. M.
    1960    *Acoustic theory of speech production* (The Hague, Mouton).

Geist, F. D.
1961 "Nasal cavity, larynx, mouth and pharynx", in C.G. Hartman, ed., *Anatomy of the rhesus monkey* (New York, Hafner).

Greenewalt, C. H.
1967 *Bird song: Acoustics and physiology* (Washington D. C., Smithsonian).

Henke, W. L.
1966 "Dynamic articulatory model of speech production using computer simulation", PhD. thesis, Department of Electrical Engineering, M.I.T., Cambridge, Mass.

Koenig, W., H. K. Dunn and L. Y. Lacy
1946 "The sound spectograph", *Journal of the Acoustical Society of America*, 17, 19-49.

Liberman, A. M., F. S. Cooper, D. P. Shankweiler and M. Studdert-Kennedy
1967 "Perception of the speech code", *Psychological Review*, 74, 431-461.

Lieberman, P., D. L. Klatt and W. A. Wilson
1969 "Vocal tract limitations on the acoustic repertoires of rhesus monkey and other non-human primates", in *Status Report SR*-15, Haskins Laboratories, New York City.

Marler, P. F. and W. J. Hamilton
1966 *Mechanisms of animal behavior* (New York, Wiley).

Negus, V. E.
1949 *The comparative anatomy and physiology of the larynx* (London, Hafner).

Reynolds, P. C.
1968 "Evolution of primate vocal-auditory communication systems", *American Anthropologist*, 70, 300-308.

Rowell, T. E. and R. A. Hinde
1962 "Vocal communication by the rhesus monkey (*Macaca mulatta*)", *Proceedings of the Zoological Society of London*, 138, 279-294.

Thorpe, W. H.
1961 *Bird Song* (Cambridge, Cambridge University Press).

Zhinkin, N. I.
1963 "An application of the theory of algorithms to the study of animal speech-methods of vocal intercommunication between monkeys", in R. G. Busnel, ed., *Acoustic behavior of animals* (Amsterdam, Elsevier).

# ON THE SPEECH OF NEANDERTHAL MAN*

PHILIP LIEBERMAN AND EDMUND S. CRELIN**

## INTRODUCTION

Language is undoubtedly the most important factor that differen-
tiates man from other animals. Language is, in itself, a system of
abstract logic; it allows man to extend his rational ability. Indeed,
it has often been virtually equated with man's abstract logical ability (Chomsky [1966]). It is therefore of great interest to know when
a linguistic ability similar to that of modern Man evolved. One of
the most important factors in determining the form of man's linguistic ability is his use of 'articulate' speech. We will discuss the
speech ability of an example of Neanderthal man, the La Chapelle-
aux-Saints fossil, in the light of its similarity to certain skeletal features in newborn humans. We herein use the term 'Neanderthal' as
referring to the so-called classic Neanderthal man of the Würm or
last glacial period.[1]

* We thank Professors W. Henke and D. H. Klatt for providing the computer
program and suggesting some of the supralaryngeal area functions in the speech
synthesis procedure. We also would like to thank Professors H. V. Vallois, J. E.
Pfeiffer, D. Pilbeam, W. S. Laughlin, W. W. Howells, and F. Bordes and Dr. K.
P. Oakley for many helpful comments, as well as Drs. Y. Coppens and J. L.
Heim of the Musée de L'Homme for making the La Chapelle-aux-Saints and
La Ferrassie fossils available. This study was supported in part by PHS grants
HD-01994, DE-01774 and AM-0499-15.
** Department of Anatomy, Yale University School of Medicine
[1] The La Chapelle-aux-Saints fossil as decribed by Boule (1911-1913) is per-
haps the archetypal example of 'classic' Neanderthal man. As Howells (1968)
notes, there is a class of classic Neanderthal fossils that can be quantitatively
differentiated from other fossil hominids. We recognize that some of these other
fossil hominids exhibit characteristics that are intermediate between classic

Our discussion essentially involves two factors. We have previously determined by means of acoustic analysis that Newborn humans, like nonhuman primates, lack the anatomical mechanism that is necessary to produce articulate speech (Lieberman [1968]; Lieberman *et al.* [1968], [1969]). That is, they cannot produce the range of sounds that characterizes human speech. We can now demonstrate that the skeletal features of Neanderthal man show that his supralaryngeal vocal apparatus was similar to that of a Newborn human. We will also discuss the status of Neanderthal man in human evolution.

## THE ANATOMICAL BASIS OF SPEECH

Human speech is essentially the product of a source, the larynx for vowels, and a supralaryngeal vocal tract transfer function. The supralaryngeal vocal tract which extends from the larynx to the lips, in effect, filters the source (Chiba and Kajiyama [1958]; Fant [1960]). The activity of the larynx determines the fundamental frequency of the vowel, whereas its formant frequencies are the resonant modes of the supralaryngeal vocal tract transfer function. The formant frequencies are determined by the area function of the supralaryngeal vocal tract. The vowels /a/ and /i/, for example, have different formant frequencies though they may have the same fundamental frequency. Sounds like the consonants /b/ and /d/ also may be characterized in terms of their formant frequencies. Consonants, however, typically involve transitions or rapid changes in their formant frequencies which reflect rapid changes in the area function of the supralaryngeal tract. The source for many consonants like /p/ or /s/ may be air turbulence generated at constrictions in the vocal tract.

A useful mechanical analog to the aspect of speech production

---

Neanderthal man and modern Man. These fossils may have possessed intermediate degrees of phonetic ability, but we will limit our discussion to the La Chapelle-aux-Saints fossil in this paper.

that is relevant to this paper is a pipe organ. The musical quality of each note is determined by the length and shape of each pipe. (The pipes have different lengths and may be open at one end or closed at both ends.) The pipes are all excited by the same source. The resonant modes of each pipe determine the pipe's 'filter' function. In human speech the phonetic qualities that differentiate vowels like /i/ and /a/ from each other are determined by the resonant modes of the supralaryngeal vocal tract.

The acoustic theory of speech production which we have briefly outlined thus relates an acoustic signal to a supralaryngeal area function and a source. It therefore is possible to calculate the range of sounds that an animal can produce if the range of supralaryngeal vocal tract area function variation is known. The phonetic repertoire can be further expanded if different sources are used with similar supralaryngeal vocal tract area functions. We can, however, isolate the constraints that the range of supralaryngeal vocal tract variation will impose on the phonetic repertoire, from the effects of different source functions. In short, we can see what limits would be imposed on the Neanderthal phonetic repertoire by his supralaryngeal vocal tract even though we can not reconstruct his larynx.

SKELETAL STRUCTURE AND SUPRALARYNGEAL VOCAL TRACT

The human Newborn specimens used in this study were six skulls, and six heads and necks completely divided in the midsagittal plane, and all of the cadavers dissected by the coauthor (E.S.C.) for his book on newborn anatomy (Crelin [1969]). The specimens of adult Man were fifty skulls, six heads and necks completely divided in the midsagittal plane, and the knowledge derived from dissections of adult cadavers made by the coauthor and his students during twenty continuous years of teaching human anatomy. The Neanderthal specimens were casts of two skulls with mandibles and an additional mandible of the fossil man from La Chapelle-aux-Saints described by Boule (1911-1913). The casts were purchased from the Museum of the University of Pennsylvania. Detailed measurements were

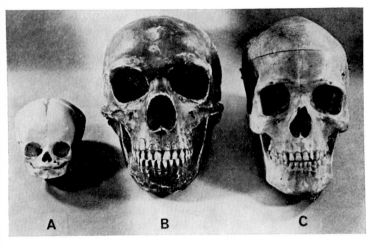

Fig. 19. Skulls of Newborn (A), and adult Man (C), and cast of Neanderthal skull (B).

made on the casts and from photographs of this fossil. The original fossil was also examined at the Musée de L'Homme in Paris by one of the authors (P.L.). Skulls of a chimpanzee and an adult female gorilla were also studied.

When the skulls of Newborn and adult Man are placed beside the cast of the Neanderthal skull there appears to be little similarity among them, especially from an anterior view (Figure 19). Much of this is due to the disparity in size, because when they are all made to appear nearly equal in size and are viewed laterally, the Newborn skull more closely resembles the Neanderthal skull than that of the adult Man (Figure 20). The Newborn and Neanderthal skulls are relatively more elongated from front to back and relatively more flattened from top to bottom than that of adult Man. The squamous part of the temporal bone is similar in the Newborn and Neanderthal (Figure 20). The fact that the mastoid process is absent in the Newborn and relatively small in the Neanderthal adds to their similarity when compared with the skull of adult Man shown in Figure 20. However, the size of the mastoid process varies greatly in adult Man. It is not unusual to find mastoid processes in normal adult

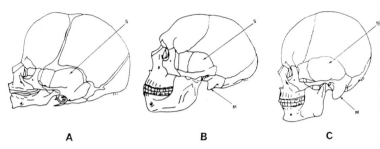

Fig. 20. Lateral views of skulls of Newborn (A), Neanderthal (B), and adult Man (C). M-Mastoid process, S-Squamous Portion of Temporal Bone.

Man as small as those of Neanderthal, especially in females. The mastoid process is absent in the chimpanzee and relatively small in the gorilla. Other features that make the Newborn and Neanderthal skulls appear similar from a lateral view are the shape of the mandible and the morphology of the base of the skull.

The Newborn and Neanderthal lack a chin, thus they share a pongid characteristic (Figure 20). The body of the Newborn and Neanderthal mandible is longer than the ramus, whereas they are nearly equal in adult Man (Figure 21). The posterior border of the Newborn and Neanderthal mandibular ramus is more inclined away from the vertical plane than that of adult Man. In Newborn and Neanderthal there is a similar inclination of the mandibular foramen leading to the mandibular canal through which the inferior

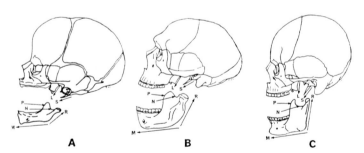

Fig. 21. Lateral views of skulls of Newborn (A), Neanderthal (B), and adult Man (C). L-Angle of Pterygoid Lamina, S-Angle of Styloid Process, P-Coronoid Process, N-Notch, R-Ramus, M-Body.

alveolar artery and nerve pass (Figure 22). The mandibular coronoid process is broad and the mandibular notch is relatively shallow in Newborn and Neanderthal (Figure 21).

The pterygoid process of the sphenoid bone is relatively short and the posterior border of its lateral lamina is more inclined away from the vertical plane in Newborn and Neanderthal when compared with adult Man (Figure 21). The styloid process is also more inclined away from the vertical plane in Newborn and Neanderthal than in adult Man (Figure 21). There are sufficient fossil remains of the Neanderthal left styloid process to determine accurately its original approximate size and inclination.

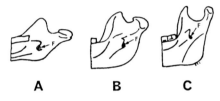

**A**          **B**          **C**

Fig. 22. Deep surface of ramus of mandible of Newborn (A), Neanderthal (B), and adult Man (C). F-Mandibular Foramen.

The dental arch of the Newborn and Neanderthal maxillas is U-shaped, a pongid feature, whereas it is more V-shaped in adult Man (Figure 23).

In the Newborn skull the anteroposterior length of the palate is less than the distance between the posterior border of the palate and the anterior border of the foramen magnum, i.e. 2.1 cm average (range 2.0-2.2 cm) and 2.6 cm average (range 2.5-2.7 cm) respectively (Figure 23). In Neanderthal the length of the palate is equal to the distance between the palate and the foramen magnum, i.e. 6.2 cm. In the skull of adult Man the length of the palate is greater than the distance between the palate and the foramen magnum, i.e. 5.1 cm average (range 4.6-5.7 cm) and 4.1 cm (range 3.6-4.9 cm) respectively. Only two of the 50 skulls of modern adult Man studied were exceptions. In one the distance between the palate and the foramen magnum was 0.4 cm greater than the length of the palate and in the other the distances were the same (4.6 cm). Note the

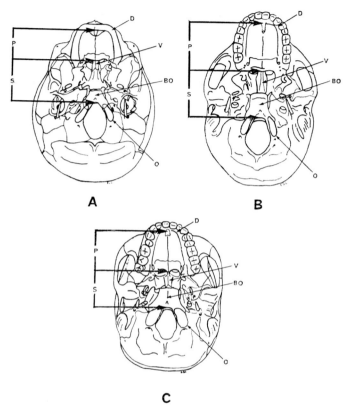

Fig. 23. Inferior views of base of skull of Newborn (A), Neanderthal (B), and adult Man (C). D-Dental Arch, P-Palate, S-Distance Between Palate and Foramen Magnum, V-Vomer Bone, BO-Basilar Part of Occipital, O-Occipital Condyle.

great absolute length of the distance between the palate and foramen magnum in Neanderthal man compared to adult Man. The relatively greater distance between the palate and the foramen magnum in the Newborn and Neanderthal when compared with adult Man is related to the similar relative size and shape of the roof of the nasopharynx in the Newborn and Neanderthal. The basilar part of the occipital bone, between the foramen magnum and the sphenoid bone, is only slightly inclined away from the horizontal toward the vertical plane (Figure 23). Therefore, the roof of the nasopharynx is a relatively shallow and elongated arch, whereas in adult Man it forms a relatively deep, short arch (Figures 26 and 27). In adult Man, without exception, the basilar part of the occipital bone is inclined more toward the vertical plane than toward the horizontal plane. Related to the shape of the roof of the nasopharynx in Newborn and Neanderthal, the vomer bone is relatively shorter in its vertical height and its posterior border is inclined away from the vertical plane to a greater degree than in adult Man (Figures 23 and 27).

In Figure 23 the foramen magnum is shown to be elongated in the anteroposterior plane in the Newborn, Neanderthal, and adult Man. Its shape is variable in both Newborn and adult Man where it frequently is more circular. The occipital condyles of Neanderthal are similar to those of the Newborn and the gorilla by being relatively small and elongated. Since the second, third and fourth cervical vertebrae of the man from La Chapelle-aux-Saints are lacking, they were reconstructed to conform with those of adult Man (Figure 24). The Neanderthal skull is placed on top of an erect cervical vertebral column instead of on one sloping forward as depicted by

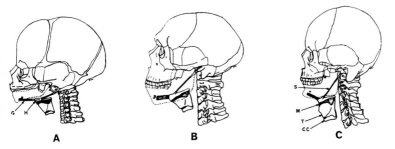

**A**                          **B**                          **C**

Fig. 24. Skull, vertebral column and larynx of Newborn (A), and adult Man (C), and reconstruction of Neanderthal (B). G-Geniohyoid Muscle, H-Hyoid Bone, S-Stylohyoid Ligament, M-Thyrohyoid Membrane, T-Thyroid Cartilage, CC-Cricoid Cartilage. Note that the inclination of the styloid process away from the vertical plane in Newborn and Neanderthal results in a corresponding inclination in the stylohyoid ligament. The intersection of the stylohyoid ligament and geniohyoid muscle with the hyoid bone of the larynx occurs at a higher position in Newborn and Neanderthal. The high position of the larynx in the Neanderthal reconstruction follows, in part, from this intersection.

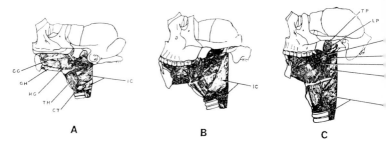

Fig. 25. Tongue and pharyngeal musculature of Newborn (A) and adult Man (C), and reconstruction of Neanderthal (B). GG-Genioglossus, GH-Geniohyoid, HG-Hyoglossus, TH-Thyrohyoid CT-Cricothyroid TP-Tensor Veli Palatini, LP-Levator Veli Palatini, SC-Superior Pharyngeal Constrictor, MC-Middle Pharyngeal Constrictor, IC-Inferior Pharyngeal Constrictor, SH-Stylohyoid SG-Styloglossus

Boule (1911-1913) and Keith (1925). This is in agreement with Straus and Cave (1957). In addition, the spinous processes of the lower cervical vertebrae shown for adult Man in Figure 24 are curved slightly upward. They are from a normal vertebral column and were purposely chosen to show that those of Neanderthal were not necessarily pongid in form. In fact, the cervical vertebral column of Neanderthal also resembles that of Newborn (Figure 24).

In order to reconstruct the supralaryngeal vocal tract of Neanderthal it was essential to locate the larynx properly. Because of the many similarities of the base of the skull and the mandible between Newborn and Neanderthal, coupled with the known detailed anatomy of Newborn, of adult Man and of apes, it was possible to do this with a high degree of confidence (Figure 24). Although the larynx was judged to be as high in position as that in Newborn and apes, it was purposely dropped to a slightly lower level to give Neanderthal every possible advantage in his ability to speak.

Once the position of the larynx in Neanderthal was determined, it was a rather straightforward process to reconstruct his tongue and pharyngeal musculature (Figure 25). The next step was to reconstruct the vocal tract of Neanderthal by building his laryngeal, pharyngeal, and oral cavities with modelling clay in direct contact with the skull cast. After this was done a silicone rubber cast was made from the clay mold of the air passages, including the nasal cavity. At the same time similar casts were made of the air passages, including the nasal cavity of the Newborn and adult Man. This was done by filling each side of the split air passages separately in the sagittally-sectioned Newborn and adult Man heads and necks to ensure perfect filling of the cavities. The casts from each side of a head and neck were then fused together to make a complete cast of the air passages.

Even though the cast of the Newborn air passages is much smaller than those of Neanderthal and adult Man it is apparent (Figure 26) that the casts of the Newborn and Neanderthal are quite similar and have pongid characteristics (Negus [1949]). When outlines of the air passages from all three are made nearly equal size, one can more readily recognize what the basic differences and similarities are (Figure 27). Although the nasal and oral cavities of Neanderthal are actually larger than those of adult Man, they are quite similar in shape to those of the Newborn in being very elongated. The high position of the opening of the larynx into the pharynx in Newborn and apes is directly related to the high position of the hyoid bone; therefore, the opening of the larynx into the pharynx

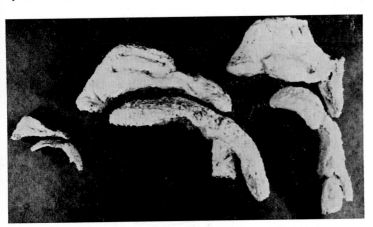

Fig. 26. Casts of air passages of Newborn (A), Neanderthal reconstruction (B) and adult Man (C). The nasal, oral, and pharyngeal air passages are shown.

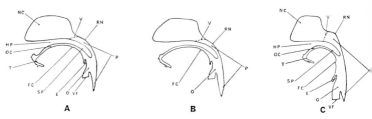

Fig. 27. Supralaryngeal air passages of Newborn (A), Neanderthal reconstruction (B), and adult Man (C). NC-Nasal Cavity, V-Vomer Bone, RN-Roof of Nasopharynx, P-Pharynx, HP-Hard Palate, SP-Soft Palate, OC-Oral Cavity, T-Tip of Tongue, FC-Foramen Cecum of Tongue, E-Epiglottis, O-Opening of Larynx into Pharynx, VF-Level of Vocal Folds.

is in a high position in Neanderthal (Figure 27). The development of the Newborn pharynx into the adult type is primarily a shift in the location of the opening of the larynx into it from a high to a low position. This is probably the result of differential growth where the posterior third of the tongue, between the foramen cecum and the epiglottis, shifts from a horizontal resting position within the oral cavity to a vertical resting position, to form the anterior wall of the oral part of the pharynx (Figure 27). In this shift the epiglottis becomes widely separated from the soft palate. Also the large posterior portion of the pharynx below the opening of the larynx in the Newborn is lost as it in large part becomes part of the acquired supralaryngeal portion.

## SUPRALARYNGEAL VOCAL TRACT LIMITS ON THE NEANDERTHAL PHONETIC INVENTORY

We cannot say much about either the laryngeal source or the dynamic control of Neanderthal man's vocal apparatus. We can, however, determine some of the limits on the range of sounds that Neanderthal man could have produced by modelling the reconstruction of his supralaryngeal vocal tract.

We measured the cross-sectional area of the Neanderthal and Newborn vocal tracts shown in Figure 26 at 0.5 cm intervals. These measurements gave us 'neutral' area functions which we perturbed

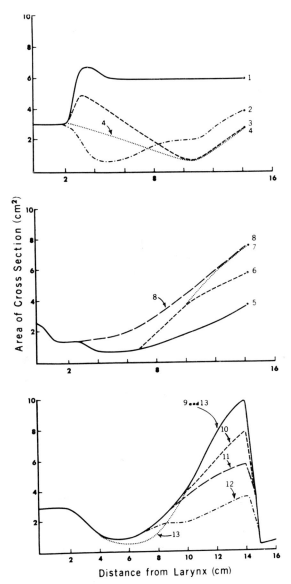

Fig. 28. Area Functions of the supralaryngeal vocal tract of Neanderthal reconstruction modelled on computer. The area function from 0 to 2 cm is derived from Fant (1960) and represents the distance from the vocal folds to the opening of the larynx into the pharynx. Curve 1 is the unperturbed tract. Curves 2, 3, and 4 represent functions directed towards a 'best match' to the human vowel /i/. Curves 5-8 are functions directed towards a 'best match' to /a/, while curves 9-13 are directed towards /u/.

towards area functions that would be reasonable if a Newborn or a Neanderthal vocal tract attempted to produce the full range of human vowels. This can be conveniently done by attempting to produce vowels that are as near as possible to /u/, /a/ and /i/ (the vowels in the words *boot, father* and *feet*). These three vowels delimit the human vowel space (Fant [1960]). We also investigated vocal tract area functions for various consonants. In all of these area functions we made use of our knowledge of the skull and muscle geometry of Man and the Neanderthal skull as well as cineradiographic data on vocalization in adult Man (Perkell [1969]); and Newborn

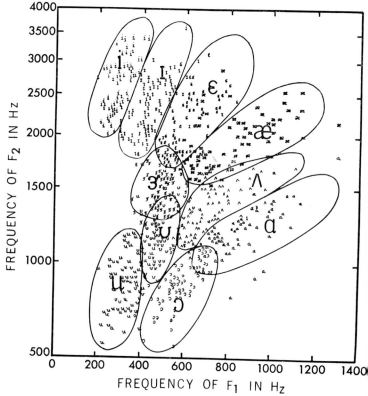

Fig. 29. Formant frequencies of American English vowels for a sample of 76 adult men, adult women and children. The closed loops enclose 90 per cent of the data points in each vowel category, after Peterson and Barney (1952).

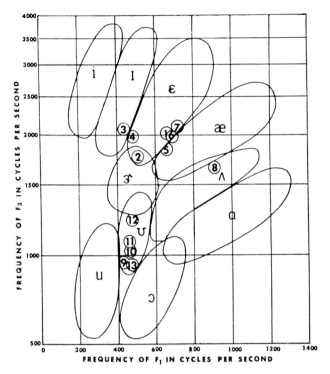

Fig. 30. Formant frequencies calculated by computer program for Neanderthal reconstruction. The numbers refer to area functions in Figure 10. The vowel loops of Figure 29 are repeated.

(Truby *et al.* [1965]). When we were in doubt as, for example, with respect to the range of variation in the area of the larynx, we used data derived from adult Man that would enhance the phonetic ability of the Neanderthal vocal tract (Fant [1960]).

Typical supralaryngeal area functions for the nonnasal portion of the Neanderthal vocal tract are plotted in Figure 28. We were able to determine what sounds would result from these area functions by using them to control a computer-implemented analog of the supralaryngeal vocal tract.

The computer program represented the supralaryngeal vocal tract by means of a series of contiguous cylindrical sections, each of fixed area. Each section can be described by a characteristic impedance and a complex propagation constant, both of which are well-known quantities for uniform cylindrical tubes. Junctions between sections satisfy the constraints of continuity of pressure and conservation of volume velocity (Henke [1966]). In this fashion the computer program calculated the three lowest formant frequencies of the vocal tract filter system which specify the acoustic properties of a vowel (Chiba and Kajiyama [1958]; Fant [1960]).

In Figure 29 the first and second formant frequencies of the vowels of American English are plotted for a sample of 76 adult men, women, and children (Peterson and Barney [1952]). The labelled closed loops enclose the data points that accounted for 90 per cent of the samples in each vowel category. The points plotted in Figure 30 represent the formant frequencies that corresponded to our simulated Neanderthal vocal tract. We have duplicated the vowel 'loops' of Figure 29 in Figure 30. Note that the Neanderthal vocal tract cannot produce the range of sounds plotted for the human speakers in Figure 29. We have compared the formant frequencies of the simulated Neanderthal vocal tract with this comparatively large sample of human speakers, since it shows that the speech deficiencies of the Neanderthal vocal tract are different in kind from the differences that characterize different human speakers, even when the sample includes adult men, adult women, and children. The acoustic vowel space of American English would not appear to be anomalously large compared to other languages although exhaustive acoustic data is lacking for many languages (Chiba and Kajiyama [1958]; Fant [1960]). It is not necessary to attempt to simulate the sounds of all languages with the computer implemented Neanderthal vocal tract since the main point that we are trying to establish is whether Neanderthal man could produce the full range of human speech. Figures 29 and 30 show that the Neanderthal vocal tract cannot produce the full range of American English vowels. Note the absence of data points in the vowel loops for /u/, /i/, /a/ and /ɔ/ in Figure 30. Since all human speakers can inherently produce all the vowels of American English, we have established that the Neanderthal phonetic repertoire is inherently limited. In some instances we generated area functions that would be appropriately humanlike, even though we felt that we were forcing the articulatory limits of the reconstructed Neanderthal vocal tract, e.g. functions 3, 9 and 13 in Figure 28. However, even with these articulatory gymnastics the Neanderthal vocal tract could not produce the vowel range of American English. The computer simulation was also used to generate consonantal vocal tract functions. It indicated that the Neanderthal vocal tract was limited to labial and dental consonants like /b/ and /d/.

The Neanderthal vocal tract also might lack the ability to produce nasal versus nonnasal distinctions. In human speech the nasal cavity acts as a parallel resonator when the velum of the soft palate is lowered, e.g. in the initial consonant of the word *mat*. The parallel resonator introduces energy minima into the acoustic spectrum and widens the bandwidths of formants (Fant [1960]). In the Neanderthal vocal tract the posterior pharyngeal cavity which leads to the oesophagus will act as a parallel resonator whether or not the nasal cavity is coupled to the rest of the vocal tract. The energy minima associated with the parallel pharyngeal resonator, however, occur at rather high frequencies, and it is not clear whether they will have a perceptual effect. Our computer simulation did not allow us to introduce parallel resonators so we could not investigate this phenomenon quantitatively. It is possible that all Neanderthal vocalizations had a 'nasal' or 'seminasal' quality.

We modelled the Newborn vocal tract in the same manner as the Neanderthal vocal tract. The computer output of the Newborn vocal tract was in accord with instrumental analyses of Newborn cry and perceptual transcriptions of Newborn vocalizations (Lieberman *et al.* [1968]). The modelling of the Newborn vocal tract thus served as a control on the way in which we estimated the range of supralaryngeal area functions and the synthesis procedure. If we had not been able to synthesize the full range of Newborn vocalizations, we would have known that we were underestimating the range of supralaryngeal vocal tract variation. Since we followed the same procedures for the Neanderthal and Newborn vocal tracts and indeed 'forced' the Neanderthal vocal tract to its limits, it is reasonable to conclude that we have not underestimated the phonetic range of the reconstructed Neanderthal vocal tract.

Our computer simulation thus shows that the supralaryngeal vocal tract of Neanderthal man was inherently incapable of producing the range of sounds that is necessary for the full range of human speech. Neanderthal man could not produce vowels like /a/, /i/, /u/ or /ɔ/ (the vowel in the word *brought*) nor could he produce consonants like /g/ or /k/. All of these sounds involve the use of a variable pharyngeal region like Man's where the dorsal part of the tongue can effect abrupt and extreme changes in the cross-sectional area of the pharyngeal region, independent of the oral region.[2] The area functions in Figure 18 are typical of the human vowels /a/, /u/ and /i/.

The Neanderthal vocal tract, however, has more 'speech' ability than the nonhuman primates. The large cross-sectional area function variations that can be made in the Neanderthal oral region make this possible since the Neanderthal mandible has no trace of a simian shelf (Boule [1911-1913]) and the tongue is comparatively thick. It can produce vowels like /I/, /e/, /U/ and /ae/ (the vowels in the words *bit*, *bet*, *but* and *bat*) in addition to the reduced schwa vowel (the first vowel in *about*). Dental and labial consonants like /d/, /b/, /s/, /z/, /v/ and /f/ are also possible although nasal versus nonnasal contrasts may not have been possible. If Neanderthal man were able to execute the rapid, controlled articulatory maneuvers that are necessary to produce these consonants and had the neural mechanisms that are necessary to perceive rapid formant transitions (special neural mechanisms appear to be involved in Man (Whitfield [1969]; Lieberman *et al.* [1967]), he would have been able to communicate by means of sound. Of course, we do not know whether Neanderthal man had these neural skills; however, even if he were able to make optimum use of his speech-producing apparatus, the constraints of his supralaryngeal vocal tract would make it im-

---

[2]  Several studies (Negus 1949, DeBrul 1958, Coon 1966) have suggested that the evolution of the human pharyngeal region played a part in making 'articulate' speech possible. Negus (1949) indeed presents a series of sketches based on reconstructions by Arthur Keith where he shows a high laryngeal position for Neanderthal man.

possible for him to produce 'articulate' human speech, i.e. the full range of phonetic contrasts employed by modern man.

## ON THE EVOLUTIONARY STATUS OF NEANDERTHAL MAN: SPEECH APPARATUS, BRAIN AND LANGUAGE

Of all the living primates only man has an extensive supralaryngal region that allows all of the intrinsic and extrinsic pharyngeal musculature to function at a maximum for speech production by changing the shape of the supralaryngeal vocal tract (Negus [1949]). It appears that the ontological development of the vocal apparatus in Man is a recapitulation of his evolutionary phylogeny.[3] If so, Nean-

---

[3] Apart from the absence of brow ridges and certain other specializations, the total form of the Newborn and Neanderthal skulls makes them members of the same class with respect to adult modern Man. The various anatomical features that we have discussed indicate this similarity but the total similarity of the complex form is most evident to the human pattern recognizer. Human observers are still the best 'pattern recognition systems' that exist. Modern statistical and computer techniques, while they are often helpful, have yet to achieve the success of human observers whether music, speech, or 'simple' visual forms like cloud patterns form the input. Both the Neanderthal and the Newborn skulls have a 'flattened out' base where there is space for the larynx to assume a high position with respect to the palate. The anatomical similarities between Newborn and Neanderthal skulls are also evident in the La Ferrassie I and Monte Circeo skulls as well as the La Quina child's skull (estimated age 8 years). The La Quina skull, which lacks the massive brow ridges of the adult Neanderthal skulls, retains the anatomical features that result in a flattened out base. These similarities, of course, recall Haeckel's 'Law of Recapitulation' (Haeckel [1907]). Neanderthal man and modern Man probably had a common ancestor who had a flattened out skull base and a high laryngeal position, but who lacked massive brow ridges. The skulls of Newborn modern man and the La Quina Neanderthal child both point to this common ancestor insofar as they lack massive brow ridges though they retain the aforementioned similarities. Classic Neanderthal man and the ancestors of modern man diverged. The massive brow ridges of adult Neanderthal man reflect this divergence. They are a specialization of Neanderthal man. We do not find any trace of brow ridges in Newborn modern man since classic Neanderthal man is not a direct ancestor of modern man. He perhaps is a 'cousin'. The evidence which many scholars have interpreted as a general and complete refutation of Haeckel's theory should be reconsidered. The process of mutation and natural selection, of necessity, results in many variations. It is not surprising to find the presence of what appear to be many fossil species that are not in the direct line of human evolution. There is no

derthal was an early offshoot from the mainstream of hominids that evolved into modern Man, just as Boule (1911-1913) recognized. It is unlikely that Neanderthal man can represent a specialized form of modern Man (Coon [1966]) or an extremely specialized species that evolved from *Homo sapiens* (Leakey and Goodall [1969]).

Natural selection would act for the retention of mutations that developed a pharyngeal region like Man's because these developments increase the number of 'stable' acoustic signals that can be used for communication. The sounds used in human language tend to be acoustically 'stable'. They are the result of supralaryngeal vocal tract configurations where deviations from the 'ideal' shape result in signals that do not differ greatly from the acoustic signals that the ideal shape produces (Stevens [forthcoming]). Errors in articulation thus have minimal effect on the acoustic character of the signal. The vowels /a/, /i/ and /u/ are the most stable vowels. The Neanderthal supralaryngeal vocal tract cannot produce these vowels which involve a variable pharyngeal region and the associated musculature (Figures 25, 27 and 18). The descent of the larynx to its lower position in adult Man thus would follow from the advantages this confers in communication. The adult human laryngeal position is not advantageous for either swallowing or respiration. The shift of the larynx from its position in Newborn and Neanderthal is advantageous for acquiring articulate speech but has the disadvantage of greatly increasing the chances of choking to death when a swallowed object gets lodged in the pharynx. In this respect nonhuman primates also have anatomical advantages (Negus [1949]). The only function for which the adult vocal human tract is better suited is speech.

In our synthesis procedure we made maximum use of the reconstructed Neanderthal vocal tract. This perhaps yielded a wider range

---

reason to assume that all of the evolutionary hominid 'experiments' are direct ancestors of modern Man, or that all fossil species of elephants are direct ancestors of modern elephants, etc. Many discussions of Haeckel's theory implicitly make this erroneous assumption when they review ontogenetic and phylogenetic data. Ontogenetic evidence can provide valuable insights into the evolution of living species.

of sounds than Neanderthal man actually produced. It is possible, however, that Neanderthal man, who had a large brain, also made maximum use of his essentially nonhuman vocal tract to establish vocal communication. This would provide the basis for mutations that lowered the larynx and expanded the range of vocal communication in modern Man's ancestral forms.

Whether or not he did possess this mental ability may never be known. A fairly good intracranial cast was made from the La Chapelle-aux-Saints fossil (Boule and Vallois [1957]). Although Neanderthal has a cranial capacity equal to that of modern Man, this cannot be regarded as a reliable indicator of his mental ability. Cranial capacity varies greatly in modern Man and cannot be correlated with individual mental ability. There are indications that Neanderthal may not have had a sufficiently developed brain for articulate speech since his brain, although large, had relatively small frontal lobes (Figure 31). From the developmental and phylogenetic viewpoints, it is the differences in the frontal lobes that distinguish most especially the human from the subhuman brain (Crosby et al. [1962]). Although the frontal lobes of the Newborn are well developed, the brain has some grossly primitive features (Crelin [1969]).

The incline of the basilar part of the occipital bone of the Newborn skull results in a corresponding incline of the adjacent brain stem away from the vertical plane to form a marked angle where it passes vertically out of the foramen magnum to become the spinal

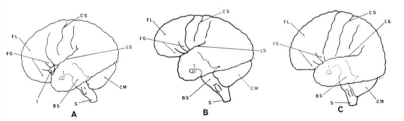

Fig. 31. Lateral view of brain of Newborn (A) and adult Man (C) and Neanderthal (B). The Neanderthal view is based on the intracranial cast of Boule and Vallois (17). FL-Frontal Lobe, FG-Inferior Frontal Gyrus, CS-Central Sulcus, LS-Lateral Sulcus, BS-Brain Stem, CM-Cerebellum, S-Spinal Medulla (cord), I-Insula.

medulla (cord.) In adult Man the vertically-oriented brain stem follows from the inclination of the adjacent basilar part of the occipital bone (Figure 27). Since the base of the Neanderthal skull is so similar to that of the Newborn, the brain stem was similarly inclined (Figure 31). Boule and Vallois (1957) noted that on the Neanderthal intracranial cast the lateral sulcus of the brain gaped anteriorly. They interpreted this as an exposure of the insula. If this is true, it is another similarity Neanderthal brain has to the Newborn brain. During brain development in Man the insula gradually becomes completely covered by the enlarging inferior frontal gyrus. At birth the insula is still exposed (Crelin [1969]) (Figure 31). Since the insula also becomes completely covered by the inferior frontal gyrus in apes, it is illogical that it would not do so in Neanderthal (Connolly [1950]). Therefore, the interpretation of the exposure of the insula in the Neanderthal brain is disputed.

Note that we are not claiming that neural developments played no role in the evolution of speech and language. We are simply stating that the anatomical mechanism for speech production is a necessary factor. Neural development is also necessary; the two factors together produce the conditions sufficient for the development of language. There is some evidence that indeed shows that the speech output mechanism and neural perceptual mechanisms may interact in a positive way. In recent years a 'motor' theory of speech perception has been developed (Liberman et al. [1967]). This theory shows that speech is 'decoded' by Man in terms of the articulatory maneuvers that are involved in its production. Signals that are quite different acoustically are identified as being the same by means of neural processing that is structured in terms of the anatomical constraints of Man's speech production apparatus. Signals that are acoustically similar may, in different contexts, be identified as being dissimilar by the same process. Animals like bullfrogs also 'decode' their meaningful sounds by means of detectors that are structured in terms of the anatomical constraints of their sound-producing systems (Capranica [1965]). These neural processes are species-specific and they obviously can only evolve as, or after, the species develops the ability to produce specific sounds. The brain and the anatomical structures associated with signalling thus evolve together. Enhanced signalling, i.e. phonetic ability, correlates with general linguistic ability in the living primates where modern man and the nonhuman primates are the extremes (Lieberman [1968], Lieberman *et al.* [1969]).

The articulatory maneuvers that underlie human speech constrain the entire neural embodiment of the grammar of language. The range of sounds and phonetic contrasts of speech form 'natural' dimensions that structure the phonologic, syntactic, and lexical properties of all human languages (Jakobson *et al.* [1963]; Postal [1968]; Lieberman [1970]). The hypothetical language that Neanderthal man could have employed would have been more 'primitive' in a meaningful sense than any human language. Fewer phonetic contrasts would have been available for the linguistic code.

Fully developed 'articulate' human speech and language appear to have been comparatively recent developments in Man's evolution. They may be the primary factors in the accelerated pace of cultural change. Our conclusions regarding Neanderthal man's linguistic ability, which are based on anatomical and acoustic factors, are consistent with the inferences that have been drawn from the rapid development of culture in the last 30,000 years in contrast to the slow rate of change before that period (Dart [1959]).

## CONCLUSION

Neanderthal man did not have the anatomical prerequisites for producing the full range of human speech.[4] He probably lacked some

---

[4]  Debetz (1961) in connection with attempts to explain directly the causes for the appearance of certain characteristics belonging to Homo sapiens notes that, "... the peculiarities of the skull, whose importance in the evolution of man is not in any case less important then the peculiarities in the structure of the hand and of the entire body, remain inexplicable". We have shown that some of the differences between the skull structure of 'classic' Neanderthal man and Homo sapiens are relevant to the production of the full range of human speech. Earlier unsuccessful attempts at deducing the presence of speech from skeletal structures, which are discussed by Vallois (1961), were hampered both by the absence of a quantitative acoustic theory of speech production, and suitable anatomical comparisons with living primates that lack the physical basis for articulate human speech.

of the neural detectors that are involved in the perception of human speech. He was not as well equipped for language as modern man. His phonetic ability was, however, more advanced than those of present day nonhuman primates and his brain may have been sufficiently well developed for him to have established a language based on the speech signals at his command. The general level of Neanderthal culture is such that this limited phonetic ability was probably utilized and that some form of language existed. Neanderthal man thus represents an intermediate stage in the evolution of language. This indicates that the evolution of language was gradual, that it was not an abrupt phenomenon. The reason that human linguistic ability appears to be so distinct and unique is that the intermediate stages in its evolution are represented by extinct species.

Neanderthal culture developed at a slow rate. We may speculate on the disappearance of Neanderthal man and we can note that his successors, for example, Cro Magnon man, who inhabited some of the old Neanderthal sites in the Dordogne (Boule and Vallois [1957]), had the skeletal structure that is typical of Man's speech mechanism. Neanderthal man's disappearance may have been a consequence of his linguistic - hence intellectual - deficiencies with respect to his sapiens competitors. In short, we can conclude that Man is human because he can say so.

## REFERENCES

Boule, M.
    1911-1913   "L'Homme fossile de La Chapelle-aux-Saints", p. 221. *Annales de Paleontologie* 6, 109; 7, 21, 85; 8, 1.
Boule, M. and H. V. Vallois
    1957   *Fossil Men* (New York, Dryden Press).
Capranica, R. R.
    1965   *The Evoked Vocal Response of the Bullfrog* (Cambridge, Mass., MIT Press).
Chiba, T. and M. Kajiyama
    1958   *The Vowel, Its Nature and Structure* (Tokyo, Phonetic Society of Japan).
Chomsky, N.
    1966   *Cartesian Linguistics* (New York, Harper and Row).

Connolly, C. J.
    1950   *External Morphology of the Primate Brain* (Springfield, Ill., C. C. Thomas).
Coon, C. S.
    1966   *The Origin of Races* (New York, Knopf).
Crelin, E, S.
    1969   *Anatomy of the Newborn: An Atlas* (Philadelphia, Lea and Febiger).
Crosby, E. C., T. Humphrey and E. W. Laver
    1962   *Correlative Anatomy of the Nervous System* (New York, Macmillan Co.).
Dart, R. A.
    1959. ."On the Evolution of Language and Articulate Speech", *HOMO* 10, 154-165.
Debetz, G. F.
    1961   "Soviet Anthropological Theory", in *Social Life of Early Man*. S. L. Washburn, ed. (Chicago, Aldine).
DuBrul, E. L.
    1958   *Evolution of the Speech Apparatus* (Springfield, Ill., C. C. Thomas).
Fant, G.
    1960   *Acoustic Theory of Speech Production* (The Hague, Mouton).
Henke, W. L.
    1966   "*Dynamic Articulatory Model of Speech Production Using Computer Simulation*", unpublished Doctoral dissertation, MIT.
Howells, W. W.
    1968   "Mount Carmel Man: Morphological Relationships", in *Proceedings, VIIIth Int'l Cong. Anthro. and Ethno. Sciences, Vol. I, Anthropology* (Tokyo).
Jakobson, R., M. Halle and C. G. M. Fant
    1963   *Preliminaries to Speech Analysis* (Cambridge, Mass., MIT Press).
Keith, A.
    1925   *The Antiquity of Man*, (London, Williams and Norgate).
Leakey, L. S. B. and V. V Goodall
    1969   *Unveiling Man's Origins* (Cambridge, Mass., Schenkman).
Liberman, A. M., F. S. Cooper, D. P. Shankweiler and M. Studdert-Kennedy
    1967   "Perception of the Speech Code", *Psychol. Rev.* 74, 431-461.
Lieberman, P.
    1968   "Primate Vocalizations and Human Linguistic Ability", *J. Acoust. Soc. Am.* 44, 1574-1584.
Lieberman, P.
    1970   "Towards a Unified Phonetic Theory", *Linguistic Inquiry* 1, 307-322.
Lieberman, P., K. S. Harris, P. Wolff and L. H. Russell
    1968   "Newborn Infant Cry and Nonhuman Primate Vocalizations", *Status Report* 17/18, *Haskins Laboratories*, New York City, scheduled *J. Speech and Hearing Res.*
Lieberman, P., D. H. Klatt, and W. A. Wilson
    1969   "Vocal Tract Limitations on the Vowel Repertoires of Rhesus Monkey and other Nonhuman Primates", *Science* 164, 1185-1187.

Negus, V. E.
  1949   *The Comparative Anatomy and Physiology of the Larynx* (New York, Hafner).
Perkell, J. S.
  1969   *Physiology of Speech Production; Results and Implications of a Quantitative Cineradiographic Study* (Cambridge, Mass., MIT Press).
Peterson, G. E. and H. L. Barney
  1952   "Control Methods Used in a Study of the Vowels", *J. Acoust. Soc. Am.* 24, 175-184.
Postal, P. M.
  1968   *Aspects of Phonological Theory* (New York, Harper and Row).
Stevens, K. N.
  forthcoming: "Quantal Nature of Speech", in *Human Communication, A Unified View*, E. E. David and P. B. Denes, eds. (New York, McGraw Hill).
Straus, W. L. Jr. and A. J. E. Cave
  1957   "Pathology and Posture of Neanderthal Man", *Quart. Rev. Biol.* 32, 348-363.
Truby, H. M., J. F. Bosma and J. Lind
  1965   *Newborn Infant Cry* (Uppsala, Almqvist and Wiksells).
Vallois, H. V.
  1961   "The Evidence of Skeletons", in *Social Life of Early Man*, S. L. Washburn, ed. (Chicago, Aldine).
Whitfield, I. C.
  1969   "Response of the Auditory Nervous System to Simple Time-Dependent Acoustic Stimuli", *Annals of N. Y. Acad. Sci.* 156, 671-677.

# PHONETIC ABILITY AND RELATED ANATOMY OF THE NEWBORN AND ADULT HUMAN, NEANDERTHAL MAN AND THE CHIMPANZEE

PHILIP LIEBERMAN, EDMUND S. CRELIN* AND DENNIS H. KLATT**

Human language is one of the defining characteristics of modern man. Although the evolution of human language has been the subject of hundreds of books and essays, not much is presently known. In recent years the primary focus has been directed towards the nature of the mental ability that may underlie the syntactic and semantic aspects of human language.[1] This follows from a rather common opinion concerning language, i.e. that its phonetic aspect is trivial and indeed finally irrelevant to the serious study of human language and its evolution. Simpson (1966) 473, for example, reviewing attempts to trace the evolution of language, notes that,

Audible signals capable of expressing language do not require any particular phonetic apparatus, but only the ability to produce sound, any sound at all. Almost all mammals and a great number of other animals can do that. Moreover, a number of animals, not only birds but also some mammals, can produce sounds recognizably similar to those of human language, and yet their jaws and palates are radically nonhuman.

Simpson essentially sets forth two premises. First, that any arbitrary set of sounds serve as a phonetic base for human language. Second, that many animals also can produce the sounds that, in fact,

* Department of Anatomy, Yale University School of Medicine, New Haven, Conn. 06510.
** Massachusetts Institute of Technology and Research Laboratory of Electronics, Cambridge, Mass. 02139.
[1] Hewes (1971) has compiled a comprehensive annotated bibliography on the evolution of language. With the exception of studies like Hockett (1960) and Hockett and Altmann (1968), most of the emphasis has been placed on the cognitive aspects of language.

occur in human language. If Simpson's premises were true there would be little point in attempting to trace the evolution of human linguistic ability by studying either the comparative phonetic abilities of modern man and other living animals, or in attempting to reconstruct the phonetic abilities of extinct fossil hominids from their skeletal remains. Neither premise, however, is true. The results of research on the perception of human speech have shown that human language depends on the existence of the particular sounds of human speech. No other sounds will do. The results of recent research on the anatomic basis of human speech have likewise demonstrated that no living animal, other than modern man, has the vocal mechanism that is necessary to produce the sounds of human speech.

We have discussed some of the anatomical factors that prevent living non-human primates and newborn humans from producing the range of sounds that characterize human speech (Lieberman [1968]; [1969]; Lieberman et al. [1968], [1969]).[2] We have also been able to reconstruct the vocal apparatus of 'classic' Neanderthal man (Lieberman and Crelin [1971]). Our present paper has two objectives. We shall compare the anatomy and speech producing ability of the vocal mechanism of adult modern man with adult chimpanzee, newborn modern man, and the reconstructed vocal mechanism of adult 'classic' Neanderthal man. We will then discuss the speech perceiving and general linguistic abilities of chimpanzee and Neanderthal man in the light of their sound making abilities. We shall, in this regard, consider some recent theoretical and experimental studies that relate the production and the perception of speech.

---

[2]    These results are consistent with the fact that it has never been possible to train a non-human primate to talk. Kellogg (1968) reviews a number of recent attempts at raising chimpanzees as though they were children. It is interesting to note that similar attempts date back to at least the eighteenth century (La Mettrie [1747]). The 'speech' of 'talking' birds is not similar to human speech at the acoustic or anatomic levels (Greenwalt [1967]). A parrot's imitation of human speech is similar to a human's imitation of a siren. The signal is accepted as a mimicry. It has different acoustic properties than the siren's signal, and it is produced by a different apparatus.

## ACOUSTIC THEORY OF SPEECH PRODUCTION

The acoustic theory of speech production (Chiba and Kajiyama [1958]; Fant [1960]) relates the vocal mechanism to the acoustic signal. Human speech essentially involves the generation of sound by the mechanism of vocal cord vibration and/or air turbulence, and the acoustic shaping of these sound sources by the resonances of the supralaryngeal vocal tract. The shape of the human supralaryngeal vocal tract continually changes during the production of speech. These changes in the supralaryngeal vocal tract change its resonant properties. A useful mechanical analog to the aspect of speech production that is of concern to this discussion is a pipe organ. The musical function of each pipe is determined by its length and shape. (The pipes have different lengths and may be open at one end or closed at both ends.) The pipes are all excited by the same source. The resonant modes of each pipe determine the note's acoustic character. In human speech the phonetic properties that differentiate vowels like [i] and [a] from each other are determined by the resonant modes of the supralaryngeal vocal tract. The frequencies at which resonances occur are called 'formant' frequencies.

The acoustic theory of speech production which we have briefly outlined thus relates an acoustic signal to a supralaryngeal vocal tract configuration and a source. It is therefore possible to determine some of the constraints of an animal's phonetic range if the range of supralaryngeal vocal tract variation is known. The phonetic repertoire of an animal can obviously be expanded if different sources are used with similar supralaryngeal vocal tract configurations. We can, however, isolate the constraints that the range of supralaryngeal vocal tract variation will impose on the phonetic repertoire.

## VOCAL TRACT ANATOMY

The anatomic specializations of modern man that are necessary for human speech are evident when we compare the supralaryngeal vocal tract of adult man with creatures who lack human speech. We

will start with a brief account of the skeletal similarities between
Neanderthal man and newborn modern man[3] and adult chimpanzee that make it possible to reconstruct the supralaryngeal vocal
tract of Neanderthal man.

[3]   The similarity between human newborn and the adult Neanderthal fossil
conforms to the view that modern man and Neanderthal man had a common
ancestor. Darwin in *On the Origin of Species* (1859), 449, clearly states the premise that we are following in making this inference. He states that "In two
groups of animals, however much they may at present differ from each other in
structure and in habits, if they pass through the same or similar embryonic stages, we may feel assured that they have both descended from the same or nearly
similar parents, and are therefore in that degree closely related." The adult
Neanderthal skull has certain specialized features, like a supraorbital torus, that
are not present in newborn modern man nor in adult modern man. This indicates that Neanderthal man is probably not directly related to modern man. He
is, as Boule (1911-1913) recognized, probably an early offshoot from the mainstream of hominids that evolved into modern man. The skulls of present day
newborn apes are quite similar to the human newborn (Schultz [1968]). This
would indicate an early common ancestral form for both present day apes and
man. It does not show that modern man has evolved by retaining infantile characteristics. Adult modern man, in his own way, deviates as much from his newborn state (Crelin [1969]); Lieberman and Crelin [1971]) as adult living apes do
from their newborn form.
    Physical anthropologists and anatomists have noted, over the years, that mea-
surements of particular aspects of Neanderthal skulls fall within the range of
variation that may be found in modern man (Patte [1955]). This finding is not
surprising since all adult modern men develop from the newborn morphology
which has many similarities to that of adult 'classic' Neanderthal man. The
course of human maturation is not even and some individuals fail to develop
'normally'. In extreme pathologic conditions like Down's Syndrome the individual may, in fact, retain many aspects of the newborn morphology, especially
those of the skull. Benda (1969) notes that Down's Syndrome may be characterized, in part, as a developmental problem. We have examined a number of
subjects afflicted with Down's Syndrome who cannot produce 'articulate' speech
(Lieberman and Crelin, unpublished data). Some of these subjects may lack the
mental ability that is necessary to control their vocal apparatus, but some of
them appear to have vocal tracts that resemble the normal newborn vocal tract.
They, in effect, have Neanderthaloid vocal tracts and they cannot produce human speech. The base of their skulls and their mandibles generally resemble
those of a Neanderthal. It is therefore not surprising that Virchow (1872) believed that the original Neanderthal skull which was found in 1856, was either
a pathologic specimen or the skull of an imbecile.
    It is also evident that different population groups of modern man have some-
what different skeletal features. In some population groups a particular skeletal
feature will fall within the range characteristic of classic Neanderthal man.

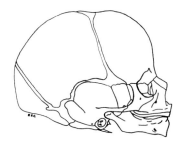

Fig. 32. Skull of a human newborn.

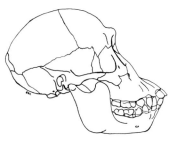

Fig. 33. Skull of an adult chimpanzee.

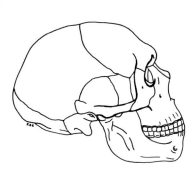

Fig. 34. Skull of the La Chapelle-aux-Saints fossil Neanderthal man.

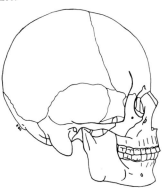

Fig. 35. Skull of an adult man.

In Figures 32-35 lateral views of the skulls of newborn man, adult chimpanzee, the La Chapelle-aux-Saints Neanderthal man, and adult modern man are presented. The skulls have all been drawn to

Laughlin (1963), for example, notes that the breadth of the ramus of the mandible in Eskimos and Aleuts can exceed the breadth of this feature in Neanderthal man. The length of the body of the mandible is also somewhat longer for Aleuts and Eskimos than is the case for other modern human skulls. The length of the body of the mandible can be about 20 percent greater than the ramus in an adult male Aleut skull. This value is, however, much smaller than is the case for either Neanderthal man or newborn human where the length of the body of the mandible is 60 to 100 percent greater than the ramus (as measured on a lateral projection to the midline of the mandible). The total ensemble of skeletal features of the base of the skull for Aleuts and Eskimos is, moreover, consistent with the 'angulation' of the vocal tract of adult modern man.

appear nearly equal in size. Skull features of the newborn, the chimpanzee, and Neanderthal man that are similar to each other, but different from that of adult modern man, are as follows: (A) a generally flattened out base, (B) lack of mastoid processes (very small in Neanderthal), (C) lack of a chin (occasionally present in the newborn), (D) the body of the mandible is much longer than the ramus (about 60 to 100 per cent longer), (E) the posterior border of the mandibular ramus is markedly slanted away from the vertical plane, (F) a more horizontal inclination of the mandibular foramen leading to the mandibular canal, (G) the pterygoid process of the sphenoid bone is relatively short and its lateral lamina is more inclined away from the vertical plane, (H) the styloid process is more inclined away from the vertical plane, (I) the dental arch of the maxilla is U-shaped instead of V-shaped, (J) the basilar part of the occipital bone between the foramen magnum and the sphenoid bone is only slightly inclined away from the horizontal toward the vertical plane, (K) the roof of the nasopharynx is a relatively shallow elongated arch, (L) the vomer bone is relatively short in its vertical height and its posterior border is inclined away from the vertical plane, (M) the vomer bone is relatively far removed from the junction of the sphenoid bone and the basilar part of the occipital bone, (N) the occipital condyles are relatively small and elongated.

The chimpanzee differs from the newborn and adult modern man and Neanderthal man insofar as its mandible has a 'simian shelf', i.e. internal buttressing of the anterior portion of mandible. The simian shelf inhibits the formation of a large air cavity behind the teeth. In adult man a large cavity behind the teeth can be formed by pulling the tongue back in the mouth.

The significance of these skeletal features can be seen when the supralaryngeal vocal tracts that correspond to these skulls are examined. The chimpanzee specimen used in this study was the head and neck of a young adult male sectioned in the midsagittal plane (Figure 36). The human newborn and adult specimens were those described by Lieberman and Crelin (1971) which included a number of heads divided in the midsagittal plane. Silicone-rubber casts were made of the air passages, including the nasal cavity, of the

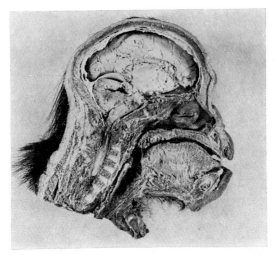

Fig. 36. Left half of the head and neck of a young adult male chimpanzee
sectioned in the midsaggital plane.

chimpanzee, newborn and adult man. This was done by filling each
side of the split air passages separately in the sectioned heads and
necks to insure perfect filling of the cavities. The casts from each
side of a head and neck were then fused together to make a complete
cast of the air passages. The cast of the Neanderthal air passages
was made from the reconstructed nasal, oral, pharyngeal and laryngeal cavities of the La Chapelle-aux-Saints fossil (Lieberman and
Crelin [1971]). All four casts are shown in the photograph in Figure
37.

Even though the cast of the newborn air passages is much smaller
than those of chimpanzee and adult modern man and Neanderthal
man it is apparent that the casts of newborn and chimpanzee are
quite similar. When outlines of the air passages from all four are
made nearly equal in size in Figure 38, one can more readily recognize what the basic differences and similarities are. (1) Newborn
human, the chimpanzee, and Neanderthal man all have their tongue
at rest completely within the oral cavity, whereas in adult man the
posterior third of the tongue is in a vertical position forming the
anterior wall of the supralaryngeal pharyngeal cavity. The foramen

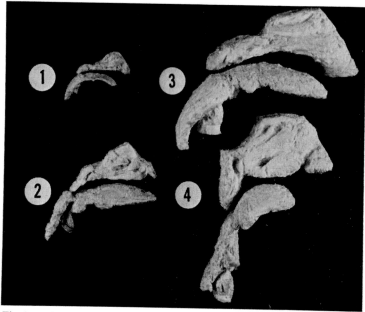

Fig. 37. Casts of the nasal, oral, pharyngeal, and laryngeal cavities of (1) new-born human, (2) adult chimpanzee, (3) Neanderthal reconstruction and (4) adult human.

cecum of the tongue is thus located far more anteriorly, in the oral cavity, in chimpanzee and newborn than it is in adult man. (2) In the newborn, chimpanzee and Neanderthal the soft palate and epi-glottis can be approximated, whereas they are widely separated in adult man and cannot approximate. (3) There is practically no su-pralaryngeal portion of the pharynx present in the direct airway out from the larynx when the soft palate shuts off the nasal cavity in chimpanzee, Neanderthal and newborn man. In adult man half of the supralaryngeal vocal tract is formed by the pharyngeal cavity. This difference between the chimpanzee, Neanderthal, and new-born - and adult man, is a consequence of the opening of the larynx into the pharynx, which is immediately behind the oral cavity in the chimpanzee, Neanderthal and newborn. In adult man this opening occurs farther down in the pharynx. Note that the supralaryngeal pharynx in adult man serves both as a pathway for the ingestion of food and liquids and as an airway to the larynx. In chimpanzee, Neanderthal, and newborn man the section of the pharynx that is behind the oral cavity is reserved for deglutition. The high epiglottis can, moreover, close the oral cavity to retain solids and liquids and allow unhampered respiration through the nose. (4) The level of the vocal folds (cords) at rest in the chimpanzee is at the upper border of the fourth cervical vertebra, whereas in adult man it is between the fifth and sixth in a relatively longer neck. The position of the hyoid bone is high in the chimpanzee, Neanderthal and newborn. This is concomitant with the high position of the larynx.

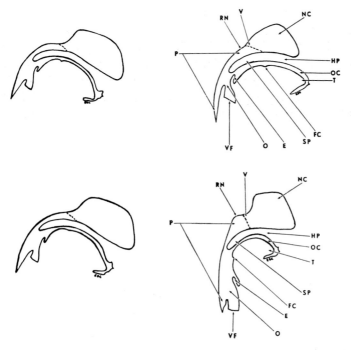

Fig. 38. Diagrams of the air passages of (a) newborn human, (b) adult chimpanzee, (c) Neanderthal man and (d) adult human. The anatomical details that are keyed on the chimpanzee and adult man are as follows: P-Pharynx, RN-Roof of Nasopharynx, V-Vomer Bone, NC-Nasal Cavity, HP-Hard Palate, OC-Oral Cavity, T-Tongue, FC-Foranen Cecum, SP-Soft Palate, E-Epiglottis, O-Opening of Larynx into Pharynx, VF-Level of Vocal Folds.

## SUPRALARYNGEAL VOCAL TRACT CONSTRAINTS ON PHONETIC REPERTOIRES

We have noted that human speech production involves a source of sound and a supralaryngeal vocal tract that acts as an acoustic 'filter' or modulator. Man uses his articulators (the tongue, lips, mandible, velum, pharyngeal constrictors, etc.) to modify dynamically in time the resonant structure that the supralaryngeal vocal tract imposes on the acoustic sound pressure radiated at the speaker's lips and nares.

The phonetic inventory of a human language is therefore limited at the articulatory level by (1) the number of acoustically distinct sound sources that man is capable of controlling during speech communication, and (2) the number of distinct resonant patterns available through positioning of the articulators and dynamic manipulation of the articulators. In most human languages, a phonetic analysis will reveal a phonemic inventory on the order of 20-40 distinct sound types (Troubetskoy [1939]; Jakobson et al. [1952]). Most of the segment proliferations are achieved through the varied use of the articulators. For example, in English there are at least ten vowels that differ primarily in the articulatory configuration of the supralaryngeal vocal tract, and concomitantly in the resonant, i.e., the formant structure of the acoustic output (Peterson and Barney [1952]).

There is a direct relationship between the articulatory configuration of the supralaryngeal vocal tract and the formant structure Fant [1960]). The relationship depends exclusively on the area function or cross-sectional area of the vocal tract as a function of the distance from the vocal cords to the lips. The availability of digital computers makes it possible to determine the range of formant frequency patterns that a supralaryngeal vocal tract can produce. If the supralaryngeal vocal tract area function is systematically manipulated in accord with the muscular and anatomical constraints of the head and neck, a computer can be programmed to compute the formant frequencies that correspond to the total range of supralaryngeal vocal tract variation (Henke [1966]). In other words, a computer-implemented model of a supralaryngeal vocal tract can be used to determine the possible contribution of the vocal tract to the phonetic repertoire. We can conveniently begin to determine whether a non-human surpralaryngeal vocal tract can produce the range of sounds that occurs in human language by exploring its vowel producing ability. Consonantal vocal tract configurations can also be modelled. It is, however, reasonable to start with vowels since the production of consonants may also involve rapid coordinated articulatory maneuvers and we can only speculate on the presence of this ability in fossil hominids.

## THE VOWEL TRIANGLE

Articulatory and acoustic analyses have shown that the three vowels [i], [a] and [u] are the limiting articulations of a vowel triangle that is language universal (Troubetzkoy [1939]). The body of the tongue is high and fronted to form a constricted oral cavity in [i] whereas it is low to form a large oral cavity in [a] and [u]. Figure 39 shows a midsaggital outline of the vocal tract for the vowels [i], [a] and [u], as well as the cross-sectional areas of the vocal tract (Fant [1960]) and the frequency domain transfer functions for these vowels (Gold and Rabiner [1968]). The tongue body forms a large pharyngeal cavity in [i] and [u] and a constricted pharyngeal cavity in [a]. If the tongue body moves to form any greater constrictions, turbulent friction noise is generated at the vocal tract constriction and the articulation produces a consonant, not a vowel. Other English vowels are produced by means of supralaryngeal vocal tract configurations within the articulatory triangle[4] defined by [i], [a] and [u].

The universality and special nature of [i], [a], and [u] can be argued from theoretical grounds as well. Employing the simplified and idealized area functions shown in Figure 40, Stevens (1969), has shown that these articulatory configurations (1) are acoustically stable for small changes in articulation and therefore require less

---

[4]   It can be argued that [ɔ] forms a fourth position on a vowel 'quadrangle', but this modification will not affect our arguments in any essential way.

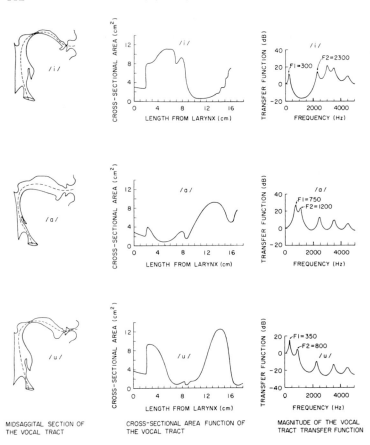

Fig. 39. Illustrations of approximate (a) midsaggital sections, (b) cross-sectional area functions and (c) accoustic transfer functions of the vocal tract for the vowels [i], [a] and [u].

precision in articulatory control than similar adjacent articulations, and (2) contain a prominent acoustic feature, i.e., 2 formants that are in close proximity to form a distinct energy concentration.

The vowels [a], [i] and [u] have another unique property. They are the only vowels in which an acoustic pattern can be related to a unique vocal tract area function (Lindblom and Sundberg [1969]; Stevens [1969]). Other vowels like [e], [I], [U] etc. can be produced by means of several alternate area functions (Stevens and House [1955]). A human listener, when he hears a syllable that contains a token of [a], [i], or [u] can calculate the size of the supralaryngeal vocal tract that was used to produce the syllable. The listener, in other words, can tell whether a speaker with a large or small vocal tract is speaking. This is not possible for other vowels since a speaker with a small vocal tract can, for example, by increasing the degree of lip rounding, produce a token of [U] that would be consistent with a larger vocal tract with less lip rounding. These uncertainties do not exist for [a], [i] and [u] since the required disconti-

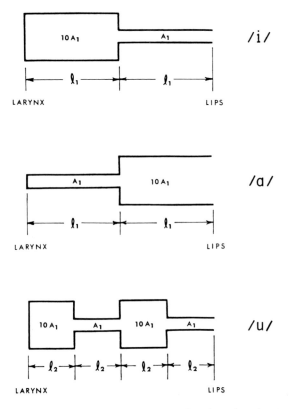

Fig. 40. Stylized supralaryngeal vocal tract area functions that characterize the human vowels [a], [i] and [u].

nuities in the supralaryngeal vocal tract area functions (Figure 39) produce acoustic patterns that are beyond the range of compensatory maneuvers. The degree of lip rounding for the u in Figure 39 is, for example, so extreme that it is impossible to constrict the lip opening any more and still produce a vowel.[5] The vowels [a], [i] and [u] are therefore different in kind from the remaining 'central' vowels. These 'vocal-tract size calibrating' properties of [a], [i] and [u] have a crucial role in the perception of speech and we will have more to say on this matter.

We can conclude from these considerations that the vowel space reserved for human language is delimited by the vowels [a], [i] and [u]. A study of the theoretical limitations on vowels produced by another related species can therefore proceed by determining the largest vowel triangle that its articulatory system is capable of generating.

THE VOWEL TRIANGLE IN CHIMPANZEE AND NEWBORN MAN
AND NEANDERTHAL MAN

Some general observations are in order before detailed consideration of the vowel producing capabilities of the chimpanzee, human newborn and Neanderthal man. The idealized area functions of Stevens (Figure 40) require a relatively large ratio of the areas of the large and small section. In addition they require rather abrupt boundaries between sections. These configurations can be approximated in adult man at the junction of the pharyngeal and oral cavities where the styloglossus muscle can be effective in pulling the body of the tongue upwards and backwards in the direction of the nasopharynx (Sobotta-Figge [1965]; Perkell [1969]; Lieberman [1970]). The cross-sectional area of the oral and pharyngeal cavities can be independently manipulated in adult man (refer to Fig. 39) while a midpoint constriction is maintained. The supralaryngeal vocal tract of adult man thus can, in effect, function as a 'two' tube system. The lack of a supralaryngeal pharyngeal region prevents the

[5]   If the size of the constriction becomes too small, turbulent noise will be generated at the constriction and the sound will no longer be a vowel.

chimpanzee, human newborn and Neanderthal from employing these mechanisms. They can only attempt to distort the tongue body in the oral cavity to obtain changes in cross-sectional areas. The intrinsic musculature of the tongue severely limits the range of deformations that the tongue body can be expected to employ. The chimpanzee, human newborn and Neanderthal man, in effect, have 'single tube' resonant systems.

The chimpanzee and human newborn heads are both smaller than adult man. This imposes a further difficulty since it makes it difficult to form the large cavities that are found in the vowels of man. Therefore comparable cavity area ratios would require the use of smaller constrictions than adult man, but this would violate the requirement of non-turbulent flow in the constricted part of the vocal tract for vowels.

### THE CHIMPANZEE VOWEL TRIANGLE

The vowel [a] could be articulated by a chimpanzee if he were to open his mandible sufficiently to obtain a flared area function. Taking into account the constraints mentioned above, an area function for a chimpanzee [a] has been estimated and plotted in Figure 41. Formant frequencies corresponding to the area function have been computed by means of an algorithm described by Henke (1966) and are tabulated in the figure. The area of the vocal tract was specified at 0.5 cm intervals using this algorithm, which was implemented on a digital computer. When the two lowest formants are scaled down in frequency by a factor proportional to the ratio of a chimpanzee vocal tract length of 10 cm to the mean vocal tract length of 17 cm of adult man, then the chimpanzee formants can be compared directly with comparable data in adult man. This is done on a plot of first formant frequency versus second formant frequency in Figure 42 where the data point for this is denoted by the circled number (1). We see that the chimpanzee formant patterns for this vowel configuration do not fall within the range of [a] data for man, but rather lie inside the vowel triangle in the [ʌ] region. The normative data for modern man with which the chimpanzee vowel is compared is derived from a sample of 76 adult men, adult women, and children (Peterson and Barney [1952]). The labelled loops enclose the data points that accounted for 90 per cent of the samples in each vowel category. The children in the Peterson and Barney study were sufficiently old that they all had vocal tracts that conformed to that typical of adult morphology (Lieberman et al. [1968]; Crelin and Lieberman, unpublished data).

The vowel [i] could be best approximated by a chimpanzee by pulling the body of the tongue forward with the mandible lowered slightly. The cross-sectional area of the back cavity will not be large, but may approach the area function estimated in Figure 41. This area function results in formant locations that are tabulated in Figure 41 and scaled and plotted in Figure 42 (data point (2)). The for-

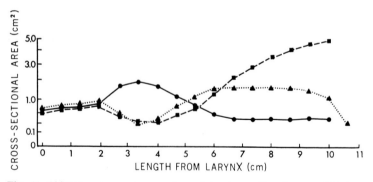

| /i/ •——• | | | /ɑ/ ■--■ | | | /u/ ▲·····▲ | | |
|---|---|---|---|---|---|---|---|---|
| Formant | Freq. | Freq./1.7 | Formant | Freq. | Freq./1.7 | Formant | Freq. | Freq./1.7 |
| 1 | 610 | 360 | 1 | 1220 | 720 | 1 | 830 | 490 |
| 2 | 3400 | 2000 | 2 | 2550 | 1500 | 2 | 1800 | 1060 |
| 3 | 4420 | 2600 | 3 | 5070 | 2980 | 3 | 4080 | 2390 |

Fig. 41. Chimpanzee supralaryngeal vocal tract area functions modelled on computer. These functions were the 'best' approximations that could be produced, given the anatomic limitations of the chimpanzee, to the human vowels [i], [a] and [u]. The formant frequencies calculated by the computer program for each vowel are tabulated and scaled to the average dimensions of the adult human vocal tract.

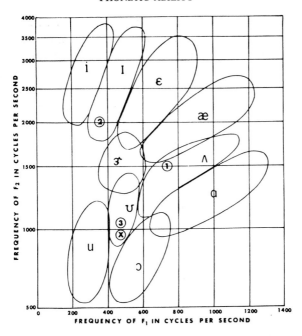

Fig. 42. Plot of formant frequencies for chimpanzee vowels of Figure 9, data points (1), (2) and (3), scaled to correspond to the size of the adult human vocal tract. Data point (X) represents an additional point for human newborn. The closed loops enclose 90 percent of the data points derived from a sample of 76 adult men, women, and children producing American-English vowels (Peterson and Barney [1952]). Note that the chimpanzee and newborn vocal tracts cannot produce the vowels [i], [u] and [a].

mants do not fall within the [i] region in adult man but rather inside the vowel triangle in the [I] region.

The vowel [u] is virtually impossible for the chimpanzee to articulate. A large front cavity requires the mandible to be lowered because the simian shelf prevents the tongue body motion found in man. However, the required lip rounding is incompatible with a lowered mandible. An approximation to a chimpanzee [u] area function is estimated in Figure 41. Again, the formant locations of this area function are computed, scaled, and plotted in Figure 42 (data point 3). They indicate that the comparable English vowel is [U] and not [u].

The discussion of the vowel triangle has not considered the effects of the chimpanzee pharynx, which acts as a relatively short side-branch resonator. The pharyngeal section may be essentially closed in a back vowel such as [a], but it probably plays an important role in [i]. The presence of a side-branch resonator has the effect of modifying formant locations and also the effect of introducing anti-resonances into the vocal tract transfer function. We estimate that the lowest frequency antiresonance for [i] of a slightly flared 6 cm pharyngeal section is about 2000 Hz.[6]

## NEWBORN HUMAN

The supralaryngeal vocal tract of the human newborn does not differ substantially from the chimpanzee's (Figures 32-34). The absence of a simian shelf in the mandible, however, allows the formation of a larger front cavity in the production of vowels that approximate the adult human [u]. In Figure 43 the formant locations of this area function, which resemble that of Figure 41 for the chimpanzee [u] approximation with a larger front cavity, are computed, scaled, and plotted as data point (X). The resulting vowel sound is comparable to the English vowel [U] not [u], but it is a closer acoustic approximation to [u]. The acoustic output of the newborn vocal tract does not otherwise differ substantially from the chimpanzee vocal tract. Perceptual and acoustic studies of the vocalizations of human newborn (Irwin [1957]; Lieberman et al. [1968]) show that all, and only the vowels that can be produced, are indeed produced.

## NEANDERTHAL MAN

The vowel producing abilities of the reconstructed supralaryngeal vocal tract of the La Chapelle-aux-Saints Neanderthal fossil are presented in Figure 43. The formant frequencies of the Neanderthal supralaryngeal vocal tract configurations that best approximated

---

[6]    This may have a perceptual effect similar to that of nasality as transfer function zeros appear in adult human speech in nasalized vowels.

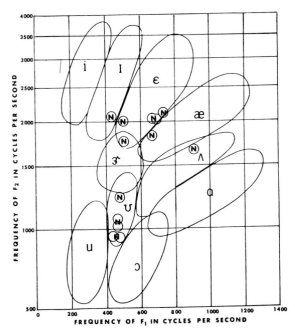

Fig. 43. Plot of first and second formant frequencies for 'extreme' vowels, data points (N), of reconstructed Neanderthal vocal tract (Lieberman and Crelin [1971]).

the human vowels [a], [i] and [u] were computed, scaled and plotted with respect to adult modern man (Lieberman and Crelin [1971]). Note that the Neanderthal vowels which are each labelled 'N' do not fall in the human ranges for [a], [i] or [u]. The Neanderthal vocal tract was given the benefit of all possible doubts in the computer modelling. The maximum range of laryngeal cavity variation typical of modern man (Fant [1960]) was, for example, used in a manner that would enhance the phonetic ability of the Neanderthal vocal tract. Articulatory maneuvers that would be somewhat acrobatic in modern man were also used to enhance Neanderthal phonetic ability. Our computer modelling was guided by the results of X-ray motion pictures of speech production, vocalization, swallowing, and respiration in adult man (Perkell [1969];

Haskins Laboratories [1962]) and in newborn (Truby et al. [1965]). This knowledge, plus the known comparative anatomy of the living primates, allowed a fairly 'conservative' simulation of the vowel producing ability of this fossil specimen who is typical of the range of 'classic' Neanderthal man[7]. We perhaps allowed a greater vowel producing range for Neanderthal man since we consistently generated area functions that were more humanlike than apelike whenever we were in doubt. Despite these compensations the Neanderthal vocal tract cannot produce [a], [i] or [u]. The absence of these vowels from the vowel systems of chimpanzee, newborn human, and Neanderthal man in Figures 42 and 43 thus is an indirect way of showing that the vocal tracts of these creatures cannot form the abrupt area functions that are necessary for these vowels. Our modelling of the newborn vocal tract served as a control procedure since we were able to produce the vowels that newborn humans actually produce. We produced, however, a greater vowel range than has been observed in the acoustic analysis of chimpanzee vocalizations (Lieberman [1968]). We will return to this point later in our discussion since it may reflect the absence of required neural, mechanisms in the nonhuman primates.

### SPEECH PRODUCTION AND SPEECH PERCEPTION

Supralaryngeal vocal tract area functions that approximated typical consonantal configurations for adult man (Fant [1960]; Perkell [1969]) were also modelled on the digital computer (Lieberman and Crelin [1971]). Chimpanzee, newborn human, and Neanderthal man all appeared to have anatomical mechanisms that would allow the production of both labial and dental consonants like [b], [p], [t], [e] etc., if other muscular and neural factors were present.

It is obvious that some of these factors are not present in new-

---

[7]   We have noted (Lieberman and Crelin [1971]) that a number of fossils, that differ slightly in other ways, all have a 'flattened-out' skull base and other anatomical features that indicate the absence of a supralaryngeal vocal tract like adult modern man's. There is, in other words, a class of 'Neanderthaloid' fossils who lack the ability to produce the full range of human speech.

born human since neither labial nor dental consonants occur in the utterances of newborn infants (Irwin [1957]). It is possible that the nonoccurrence of these consonants is a consequence of a general inability to produce rapid articulatory maneuvers. The situation is more complex in chimpanzee where a discrepancy again exists between the constraints that the supralaryngeal vocal tract imposes on the phonetic repertoire and actual performance. Chimpanzees do not appear to produce dental consonants although they have the anatomical 'machinery' that would permit them to do so. Observations of captive chimpanzees have not, for example, revealed patterns of vocal communication that utilize contrasts between labial and dental consonants (Lieberman [1968]). It is unlikely that the failure to observe dental consonants in chimpanzee vocalizations is due to a limited data sample since attempts to train chimpanzees to mimic human speech have not succeeded in teaching them to produce dental consonants. At least one chimpanzee has been taught to produce labial consonants like [p] and [m] (Hayes [1952]) so the absence of dental consonants cannot be ascribed to a general inability to produce rapid articulatory maneuvers.

Our computer modelling of the chimpanzee vocal tract shows that these animals have the anatomic ability that would allow them to produce a number of vowels that in human speech are 'phonemic' elements, i.e., sound contrasts that convey linguistically meaningful information. Chimpanzees, however, do not appear to make use of these vowel possibilities. Instead, they appear to make maximum use of the 'neutral' uniform cross-section supralaryngeal vocal tract shape (Jakobson et al. [1952]; Lieberman [1968]) with source variations. Chimpanzees, for example, will make calls that are different insofar as the glottal excitation is weak, breathy, has a high fundamental frequency,[8] etc.

The absence of sounds that are anatomically possible may perhaps reflect perceptual limitations. In other words, chimpanzees may not use dental consonants in contrast with labial consonants

[8] Meaningful chimpanzee calls can be 'seen' in context in the recent sound motion pictures taken by P. Marler at the Combe Stream Reserve chimpanzee project of Goodall (1965).

because they cannot perceptually differentiate these sounds. Differences in vowel quality as between [I] and [e], for example, may also be irrelevant for chimpanzees. The absence of the vowels [a], [i] and [u] from the chimpanzee's phonetic abilities is consistent with this hypothesis which has wider implications concerning the general phonetic and linguistic abilities of the living nonhuman primates and hominid fossils like Neanderthal man.

## SPEECH AND LANGUAGE

Linguists have, as we noted earlier, tended to ignore the phonetic level of language and speech production. The prevailing assumption is that the interesting action is at the syntactic and semantic levels, and that just about any sequence of arbitrary sounds would do for the transfer of linguistic information. Some linguists might, for example, point out that even simple binary codes, such as Morse code, can be used to transmit linguistic information. Neanderthal man, in this view, therefore would need only one sound contrast to communicate. After all, modern man can communicate by this means: why not Neanderthal man? The answer to this question is quite simple. Human speech is a special mode of communication that allows modern man to communicate at least ten times faster than any other known method. Sounds other than speech cannot be made to convey language well.[9] That knowledge comes from 55 years of trying to make nonspeech sounds for use in reading machines for the blind, that is, devices that scan the print and convert it into meaningful sounds. In spite of the most diligent efforts in connection with the development of these machines, no nonspeech acoustic alphabet has yet been contrived that can be made to work more than one-tenth as well as speech (Liberman et al. [1967]). Nor has any better degree of success attended efforts towards the use of visual displays in the development of 'hearing' machines for the deaf (Koenig et al. [1946]).

[9]  I am essentially paraphrasing the discussion presented by Liberman (1970) with regard to the linguistic status of human speech and the process of speech encoding. Liberman's logic is clear, correct and succinct.

The problem is quite clear when one considers the rate at which information is transferred in human speech. Human listeners can perceive as many as 25 to 30 phonetic segments per second in normal speech. This segment rate far exceeds the resolving power of the human auditory system. It is, for example, impossible to even count simple pulses at rates of 20 pulses per second. The pulses simply merge into a continuous tone. Communication by means of Morse code would be possible, but it would be very slow. Human speech achieves its high information rate by means of an 'encoding' process that is structured in terms of the anatomic and articulatory constraints of speech production. The presence of vowels like [a], [i] and [u] appears to be one of the anatomic factors that makes this encoding process possible.

## SPEECH ENCODING AND THE 'MOTOR THEORY' OF SPEECH PERCEPTION

In human speech a high rate of information transfer is achieved by 'encoding' phonetic segments into syllable-sized units. The phonetic representation of a syllable like [du] essentially states that two independent elements are being transmitted. The syllable [du] can be segmented at the phonetic level into two segments, [d] and [u], which can independently combine with other phonetic segments to form syllables like [di] or [gu]. Phonetic segments like [d], [g], [u] and [i] are also independent at the articulatory level insofar as these phonetic elements can each be specified in terms of an articulatory configuration. The phonetic element [u] thus involves a particular vocal tract configuration which approximates that in Figure 39. The phonetic element [d] likewise involves a particular vocal tract configuration in which the tongue blade momentarily occludes the oral cavity. It is possible to effect a segmentation of the syllable [du] at the articulatory level. If an X-ray motion picture of a speaker producing the syllable [du] were viewed it would, for example, be possible to see the articulatory gesture that produces the [d] in the syllable [du]. It is not, however, possible to segment the acoustic correlates of [d] from the speech signal.

In Figure 44, we have reproduced two simplified spectrographic patterns that will, when converted to sound, produce approximations to the syllables [di] and [du] (Liberman [1970]).[10] The dark

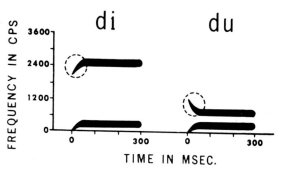

Fig. 44. Simplified spectrographic patterns sufficient to produce the syllables [di] and [du]. The circles enclose the second formant frequency transitions. (After Liberman [1970]).

bands on these patterns represent the first and second formant frequencies of the supralaryngeal vocal tract as functions of time. Note that the formants rapidly move through a range of frequencies at the left of each pattern. These rapid movements, which occur in about 50 msec, are called formant transitions. The transition in the second formant, which is encircled, conveys the acoustic information that human listeners interpret as a token of a [d] IN THE SYLLABLES [di] AND [du]. It is, however, impossible to isolate the acoustic pattern of [d] in these syllables. If tape recordings of these two syllables are 'sliced' with the electronic equivalent of a pair of scissors (Lieberman [1963]), it is impossible to find a segment that contains only [d]. There is no way to cut the tape so as to obtain a piece that will produce [d] without also producing the next vowel or some reduced approximation to it.

[10]   It can be argued that the primary acoustic cue to the identity of [d] is a brief high frequency burst of fricative noise. However adult listeners will respond correctly to the acoustic signals defined in Figure 44 even though this cue is missing.

Note that the encircled transitions are different for the two syllables. If these encircled transitions are isolated, listeners report that they hear either an upgoing or a falling frequency modulation. In context, with the acoustic correlates of the entire syllable, these transitions cause listeners to hear an 'identical' sounding [d] in both syllables. How does a human listener effect this perceptual response?

We have noted the formant frequency patterns of speech reflect the resonances of the supralaryngeal vocal tract. The formant patterns that define the syllable [di] in Figure 44 thus reflect the changing resonant pattern of the supralaryngeal vocal tract as the speaker moves the articulators from the occlusion of the tongue tip against the palate that is involved in the production of d to the vocal tract configuration of the [i]. A different acoustic pattern defines the [d] in the syllable [du]. The resonances of the vocal tract are similar as the speaker forms the initial occlusion of the [d] in both syllables; however, the resonances of the vocal tract are quite different for the final configurations of the vocal tract for [i] and [u]. The formant patterns that convey the [d] in both syllables are thus quite different since they involve transitions from the same starting point to different end points. Human listeners 'hear' an identical initial [d] segment in both of these signals because they 'decode' the acoustic pattern in terms of the articulatory gestures and the anatomical apparatus that is involved in the production of speech. The listener in this process, which has been termed the 'motor theory of speech perception' (Liberman, et al, [1967]), operates in terms of the acoustic pattern of the entire syllable. The acoustic cues for the individual 'phonetic segments' are fused into a syllabic pattern. The high rate of information transfer of human speech is thus due to the transmission of acoustic information in syllable sized units. The phonetic elements of each syllable are 'encoded' into a single acoustic pattern which is then 'decoded' by the listener to yield the phonetic representation.

In order for the process of 'motor theory perception' to work the listener must be able to determine the absolute size of the speaker's vocal tract. Similar articulatory gestures will have different acoustic correlates in different sized vocal tracts. The frequency of the first formant of [a], for example, varies from 730 to 1030 Hz in the data of Peterson and Barney (1952) for adult men and children. The frequencies of the resonances that occur for various consonants likewise are a function of the size of the speakers' vocal tract. The resonant pattern that is the correlate of the consonant [g] for a speaker with a large vocal tract may overlap with the resonant pattern of the consonant [d] for a speaker with a small vocal tract (Rand [1971]). The listener therefore must be able to deduce the size of the speaker's vocal tract before he can assign an acoustic signal to the correct consonantal or vocalic class.

There are a number of ways in which a human listener can infer the size of a speaker's supralaryngeal vocal tract. He can, for example, note the fundamental frequency of phonation. Children, who have smaller vocal tracts, usually have higher fundamental frequencies than adult men or adult women. Adult men, however, have disproportionately lower fundamental frequencies than adult women (Peterson and Barney [1952]), so fundamental frequency is not an infallible cue to vocal tract size. Perceptual experiments (Ladefoged and Broadbent [1957]) have shown that human listeners can make use of the formant frequency range of a short passage of speech to arrive at an estimate of the size of a speaker's vocal tract. Recent experiments, however, show that human listeners do not have to defer their 'motor theory' decoding of speech until they hear a two or three second interval of speech. Instead, they use the vocalic information encoded in a syllable to decode the syllable (Darwin [1971]; Rand [1971]). This may appear to be paradoxical, but it is not. The listener makes use of the formant frequencies and fundamental frequency of the syllable's vowel to assess the size of the vocal tract that produced the syllable. We have noted throughout this paper that the vowels [a], [i] and [u] have a unique acoustical property. The formant frequency pattern for these vowels can always be related to a unique vocal tract size and shape.[11] A listener,

[11]    The exact size and shape of the vocal tract can be theoretically calculated from the formant frequency pattern of these vowels if all of the theoretically infinite number of formant frequencies are known. If one, however, assumes that the formant structure of an unknown vowel is similar to [i], [u] or [a] and

when he hears one of these vowels, can thus instantly determine the size of the speaker's vocal tract. The vowels [a], [i] and [u] (and the glides [y] and [w]) thereby serve as primary acoustic calibration signals in human speech.

The anatomical impossibility for the chimpanzee to produce these vowels is thus consistent with the absence of meaningful changes in vowel quality in the vocal communications of these animals.

Chimpanzeees probably can not percieve these differences in vowel quality because they can not 'decode' specific vowels and consonants in terms of the articulatory gestures that speakers use to produce these signals. A chimpanzee on hearing a particular formant frequency pattern would, for example, not be able to tell whether it was produced by a large chimpanzee who was using an [I]-like vocal tract configuration or a smaller chimpanzee who was using an [e]-like vocal tract configuration.[12] Chimpanzees simply may not have the neural mechanism that is used in modern man to decode speech signals in terms of the underlying articulatory maneuvers. The absence of a humanlike pharyngeal region in chimpanzee is thus quite reasonable. The only function that the human supra-

---

is produced by a cavity shape shown in Figure 40, then the two lowest formants give a good estimate of vocal tract length and size. The 'quantal' nature of the speech signal discussed by Stevens (1969) makes an 'exact' knowledge of vocal tract size unnecessary for speech decoding.

[12]  The Ladefoged and Broadbent (1957) vowel perception study is very pertinent in this regard since it shows that human listeners also cannot tell whether the acoustic signal that is a token of a 'central' vowel is an [U], an [I] or an [ae] in the absence of information that tells them the size of the speaker's vocal tract. The listeners in this experiment said that the same acoustic signal 'was' the word bit, bat, or but when prior acoustic context led them to believe that the speaker had a large, medium, or small supralaryngeal vocal tract.

Note that a chimpanzee's response to simple human verbal requests does not demonstrate that the chimpanzee can 'decode' human speech. The chimpanzee may be responding to acoustic factors that are not primary linguistic units, e.g., the prosodic features that relate to the emotionally determined 'tone' of the speakers' voice. Psychoacoustic experiments designed to show whether nonhuman primates can 'decode' speech have so far yielded negative results. It is indeed almost impossible to get nonhuman primates to respond to auditory signals wherever they readily respond to visual signals. (Kellogg [1968]; Hewes [1971]).

laryngeal vocal tract is better adapted to is speech production, in particular the production of vowels like [a], [i] and [u]. The adult human supralaryngeal vocal tract is otherwise less well adapted for the primary vegetative functions of swallowing and respiration (Negus [1949]). It is quite easy for food to be caught in the adult human pharynx and block the entrance to the larynx with fatal consequences, whereas the high position of the laryngeal opening in chimpanzees and other nonhuman primates would allow them to breathe with food lodged in their pharynx. The efficiency of the respiratory apparatus is reduced considerably in adult human because the angulation of the airway (Figures 37 and 38), resulting from the low position of the larynx, appreciably lessens the volume of air which could pass through a straight tube of equal cross-section. The high position of the larynx in newborn human, chimpanzee, and Neanderthal man is efficient for respiration. As Kirchner (1970)[12] notes, "...the larynx of the newborn infant is, from the standpoint of position, a more efficient respiratory organ than its adult counterpart".

This suggests that the evolution of the human vocal tract which allows vowels like [a], [i] and [u] to be produced, and the widespread occurrence of these vowels in human languages reflect a parallel development of the neural and anatomic abilities that are necessary for language. This parallel development would be consistent with the evolution of other human abilities. The ability to use tools depends, for example, on both upright posture and an opposable thumb, and neural ability. As Darwin (1859), p. 194, noted, the theory of evolution through natural selection, "can act only by taking advantage of slight successive variations; she can never take a leap, but must advance by the shortest and slowest steps". We can think of a process in which mutations that enhanced vocal communication were retained. The presence of enhanced mental ability would enhance the probability of the retention through natural selection of an anatomical mutation that enhanced the phonetic repertoire and the rate of communication. The presence of enhanced anatomical phonetic ability would, in turn, increase the probability of the retention of mutations that enhanced the neural abilities that are involved in speech encoding, decoding, syntax, etc. Positive feedback would, no doubt, result from this 'circular' process. We would expect to find fossil forms like the La Chapelle-aux-Saints Neanderthal man who lacked a well developed vocal mechanism but who undoubtedly must have had a 'language'. The remains of Neanderthal culture all point to the presence of linguistic ability.[13]

Neanderthal man lacked the vocal tract that is necessary to produce the human 'vocal tract size-calibrating' vowels [a], [i] and [u]. This suggests that the speech of Neanderthal man did not make use of syllabic encoding. While communication is obviously possible without syllabic encoding, studies of alternate methods of communication in modern man show, as we noted before, that the rate at which information can be transferred is about one-tenth that of normal human speech. The principle of encoding extends throughout the grammar of human languages. The process wherein a deep phrase marker with many elementary $S$'s is collapsed into a derived surface structure may be viewed as an encoding process that is similar to the encoding that occurs between the phonetic level and speech (Liberman [1970]). A transformational grammar (Chomsky [1957], 1965]) may be viewed as a mechanism that encodes strings of semantic units into a surface structure. The derived surface string can be readily transmitted by a speaker and perceived and stored in short time span memory by a listener. There is no other reason why adult humans do not speak in short sentences like, *I saw the boy. The boy is fat. The boy fell down.* instead of the 'encoded' sentence, *I saw the fat boy who fell down.* The 'encoded' sentence can be transmitted more rapidly and it transmits the unitary reference of the single *boy* within the single breath-group (Lieberman, [1967]). It thus is likely that Neanderthal man's linguistic abilities were at best suited to communication at slow rates and at worst markedly inferior at the syntactic and semantic to modern man's linguistic ability. Neanderthal man's language is an interme-

---

[13] Note that the prior existence of a form of language is a necessary condition for the retention, through the process of natural selection, of mutations like the human pharyngeal region that enhance the rate of communication but are detrimental with regard to deglutition and respiration.

diate stage in the evolution of language. It may well have employed gestural communication as well as vocal signals (Hewes [1971]).

Human linguistic ability thus must be viewed as the result of a long evolutionaary process that involved changes in anatomical structure through a process of mutation and natural selection which enhanced speech communication.[14] Modern man's linguistic ability is necessarily, tied to his phonetic ability. Rapid information transfer through the medium of human speech must be viewed as a central property of human linguistic ability. It makes human language and human thought possible.

## ACKNOWLEDGEMENTS

We would like to thank Dr. E. L. Simons of Yale University for the chimpanzee specimen, Dr. P. F. Marler of Rockefeller University for making tape recordings and spectrograms of chimpanzee utterances available, and Drs. A. M. Liberman and C. Darwin of Haskins Laboratories and Dr. W. S. Laughlin of the University of Connecticut for their many useful comments. This work was supported, in part, by U.S. Public Health Service Grants AM-09499, HD-01994, DE-01774 and NB-04332-8.

[14] We, therefore, see the evolution of language as a process that is ultimately based on mechanisms that exist in the more 'primitive' fossil hominids. It is probable that the living apes, as well as other animals, still have similar mechanisms. Studies of animal communication therefore are relevant to the study of human linguistic ability. We obviously do not agree with the theory that bases modern man's linguistic abilities on 'unique' mechanisms that require 'discontinuities' in evolution (Lenneburg [1967]).

## REFERENCES

Benda, C. E.
  1969  *Down's Syndrome, Mongolism and Its Management* (New York, Grune and Stratton).
Boule, M.
  1911-1913  "L'Homme fossile de la Chapelle-aux-Saints", *Annales de Paleontologie*, 6, 109; 7, 21, 85; 8, 1.
Chiba, T. and M. Kajiyama
  1958  *The Vowel, Its Nature and Structure* (Tokyo, Phonetic Society of Japan).
Chomsky, N.
  1957  *Syntactic Structures* (The Hague, Mouton).
  1965  *Aspects of the Theory of Syntax* (Cambridge, Mass,. MIT Press).
Crelin, E. S.
  1969  *Anatomy of the Newborn; an Atlas.* (Philadelphia, Lea and Febiger).
Darwin, C.
  1859  *On the Origin of Species* (Facsimile edition) (New York, Atheneum).
Darwin, C.
  1971  "Ear Differences in the Recall of Fricatives and Vowels", *Quarterly J. Exp. Psychol.*, 23, 386-392.
Fant, C. G. M.
  1960  *Acoustic Theory of Speech Production* (The Hague, Mouton).
Gold, B. and L. R. Rabiner
  1968  "Analysis of Digital and Analog Formant Synthesizers", *IEEE-Trans. Audio Electroacoustics, AU*-16, 81-94.
Goodall, J.
  1965  "Chimpanzees of the Gombe Stream Reserve", in I. DeVore, ed. *Primate Behavior* (New York, Holt, Rinehart and Winston).
Greenwalt, C. A.
  1967  *Bird Song: Acoustics and Physiology*, (Washington, D. C., Smithsonian).
Haskins Laboratories
  1962  *X-Ray Motion Pictures of Speech*, Haskins Laboratories, 305 E. 43 St., New York City.
Hayes, C.
  1952  *The Ape in Our House* (New York, Harper and Brothers).
Henke, W. L.
  1966  "Dynamic Articulatory Model of Speech Production Using Computer Simulation", Doctoral dissertation, MIT (appendix B).
Hewes, G. W.
  1971  *Language Origins: A Bibliography*, Dept. of Anthropology, Univ. of Colorado, Boulder.
Hockett, C. F.
  1960  "The Origin of Speech", *Sci. Am.*, 203, 89-96.
Hockett, C. F. and S. A. Altmann
  1968  "A Note on Design Features", in T. A. Sebeok, ed., *Animal Communication* (Bloomington, Indiana Univ. Press).

Irwin, O. C.
  1957 "Speech Development in Childhood", in L. Kaiser, ed., *Manual of Phonetics* (Amsterdam, North-Holland) 403-425.
Jakobson, R., C. G. M. Fant and M. Halle
  1952 *Preliminaries to Speech Analysis* (Cambridge, Mass., MIT Press).
Kellogg, W. N.
  1968 "Communication and Language in the Home-raised Chimpanzee", *Science* 162, 423-427.
Kirchner, J. A.
  1970 *Pressman and Kelemen's Physiology of the Larynx* (Rochester, Minn. revised edition, American Academy of Ophthalmology and Otolaryngology).
Koenig, W., H. K. Dunn, and L. Y. Lacy
  1946 "The Sound Spectrograph", *J. Acoustical Society America* 17, 19-49.
Ladefoged, P. and D. E. Broadbent
  1957 "Information Conveyed by Vowels", *J. Acoust. Soc. Am.* 29, 98-104.
Laughlin, W. S.
  1963 "Eskimos and Aleuts: Their Origins and Evolution", *Science*, 142, 633-645.
La Mettrie, J. O.
  1747 *de L'Homme-machine*, A. Vartanian, ed., (Princeton, N. J., Princeton Univ. Press, 1960 critical edition).
Lenneburg, E. H.
  1967 *Biological Foundations Of Language* (New York, Wiley).
Liberman, A. M.
  1970 "The Grammars of Speech and Language", *Cognitive Psychology* 1, 301-323.
Liberman, A. M., D. P. Shankweiler and M. Studdert-Kennedy
  1967 "Perception of the Speech Code", *Psychol. Rev.* 74, 431-461.
Lieberman, P.
  1963 "Some Effects of Semantic and Grammatical Context on the Production and Perception of Speech", *Language and Speech* 6, 172-187.
  1967 *Intonation, Perception and Language* (Cambridge, Mass., MIT Press).
  1968 "Primate Vocalizations and Human Linguistic Ability", *J. Acoust. Soc. Am.* 44, 1574-1584.
  1969 "On the Acoustic Analysis of Primate Vocalizations", *Behav. Res. Meth. & Instru.*, 1, 169-174.
  1970 "Review of Perkell's (1968) *Physiology of Speech Production*", *Language Sciences* 13, 25-28.
Lieberman, P., K. S. Harris, P. Wolff and D. H. Russell
  1968 "Newborn Infant Cry and Nonhuman Primate Vocalizations", *Status Report* 17/18, Haskins Laboratories, New York City.
Lieberman, P., D. H. Klatt and W. A. Wilson
  1969 "Vocal Tract Limitations of the Vocal Repertoires of Rhesus Monkey and Other Non-human Primates", *Science* 164, 1185-1187.
Lieberman, P. and E. S. Crelin
  1971 "On the Speech of Neanderthal Man", *Linguistic Inquiry* 2, No. 2.

Lindblom B. and J. Sundberg
1969 "A Quantitative Model of Vowel Production and the Distinctive Features of Swedish Vowels", *Speech Transmission Laboratory Report* 1, Royal Institute of Technology, Stockholm, Sweden.

Negus, V. E.
1949 *The Comparative Anatomy and Physiology of the Larynx* (New York, Hafner).

Patte, E.
1955 *Les Neanderthaliens, Anatomie, Physiologie, Comparaisons* (Paris, Masson et cie.).

Perkell, J. S.
1969 *Physiology of Speech Production: Results and Implications of a Quantitative Cineradiographic Study* (Cambridge, Mass., MIT Press).

Peterson, G. E. and H. L. Barney
1952 "Control Methods Used in a Study of the Vowels", *J. Acoust. Soc. Am.* 24, 175-184.

Rand, T. C.
1971 "Vocal Tract Size Normalization in the Perception of Stop Consonants", *Status Report*, Haskins Laboratories, New Haven, Conn.

Schultz, A. H.
1968 "The Recent Hominoid Primates", in *Perspectives on Human Evolution*, S. L. Washburn and Phyllis Jay (New York, Holt, Rinehart and Winston).

Simpson, G. G.
1966 "The biological nature of man", *Science*, 152, 472-478.

Sobotta-Figge
1965 J. Sobotta and F. H. J. Figge, *Atlas of Human Anatomy*, Vol. II (New York, Hafner).

Stevens, K. N.
1969 "The Quantal Nature of Speech: Evidence from Asticulatory-Acoustic Data", in *Human Communication: A Unified View*, E. E. David, Jr. and P. B. Denes, eds. (New York, McGraw-Hill).

Stevens, K. N. and A. S. House
1955 "Development of a Quantitative Description of Vowel Articulation", *J. Acoust. Soc. Am.* 27, 484-493.

Troubetzkoy, N. S.
1939 *Principes de phonologie* (Paris, Klincksieck, 1949, Trans. J. Cantineau).

Truby, H. M., J. F. Bosma and J. Lind
1965 *Newborn Infant Cry* (Uppsala, Almqvist and Wiksells).

Virchow, R.
1872 "Untersuchung des Neanderthal-Schädels", Zeitschrift für Ethnographie 4, 157-165.

# JANUA LINGUARUM

## STUDIA MEMORIAE NICOLAI VAN WIJK DEDICATA
*Edited by C. H. van Schooneveld*
### SERIES MINOR

42. MILKA IVIĆ: Trends in Linguistics. Translated by Muriel Heppell. 1965. 260 pp.      Gld. 28.—

44. THEODORE M. DRANGE: Type Crossings: Sentential Meaninglessness in the Border Area of Linguistics and Philosophy. 1966. 218 pp.      Gld. 29.—

45. WARREN H. FAY: Temporal Sequence in the Perception of Speech. 1966. 126 pp., 29 figs.      Gld. 23.—

47. BOWMAN CLARKE: Language and Natural Theology. 1966. 181 pp.      Gld. 30.—

49. SAMUEL ABRAHAM and FERENC KIEFER: A Theory of Structural Semantics. 1966. 98 pp., 20 figs.      Gld. 16.—

50. ROBERT J. SCHOLES: Phonotactic Grammatically. 1966. 117 pp., many figs.      Gld. 20.—

51. HOWARD R. POLLIO: The Structural Basis of Word Association Behavior. 1966. 96 pp., 4 folding tables, 8 pp. graphs, figs.      Gld. 18.—

52. JEFFREY ELLIS: Towards and General Comparative Linguistics. 1966. 170 pp.      Gld. 26.—

54. RANDOLPH QUIRK and JAN SVARTVIK: Investigating Linguistic Acceptability. 1966. 118 pp., 14 figs., 4 tables.      Gld. 20.—

55. THOMAS A. SEBEOK (ED.): Selected Writings of Gyula Laziczius. 1966. 226 pp.      Gld. 33.—

56. NOAM CHOMSKY: Topics in the Theory of Generative Grammar. 1966. 96 pp.      Gld. 12.—

58. LOUIS G. HELLER and JAMES MACRIS: Parametric Linguistics. 1967. 80 pp., 23 tables.      Gld. 14.—

59. JOSEPH H. GREENBERG: Language Universals: With Special Reference to Feature Hierarchies. 1966. 89 pp.      Gld. 14.—

60. CHARLES F. HOCKETT: Language, Mathematics, and Linguistics. 1967. 244 pp., some figs.      Gld. 28.—

62. B. USPENSKY: Principles of Structural Typology. 1968. 80 pp.      Gld. 16.—

63. V. Z. PANFILOV: Grammar and Logic. 1968. 160 pp.      Gld. 18.—

64. JAMES C. MORRISON: Meaning and Truth in Wittgenstein's Tractatus. 1968. 148 pp.      Gld. 20.—

65. ROGER L. BROWN: Wilhelm von Humboldt's Conception of Linguistic Relativity. 1967. 132 pp.      Gld. 20.—

66. EUGENE J. BRIERE: A Psycholinguistic Study of Phonological Interference. 1968. 84 pp.      Gld. 14.—

67. ROBERT L. MILLER: The Linguistic Relativity Principle and New Humboldtian Ethnolinguistics: A History and Appraisal. 1968. 127 pp. Gld. 20.—

69. I. M. SCHLESINGER: Sentence Structure and the Reading Process. 1968. 172 pp. Gld. 22.—

70. A. ORTIZ and E. ZIERER: Set Theory and Linguistics. 1968. 64 pp. Gld. 12.—

71. HANS-HEINRICH LIEB: Communication Complexes and Their Stages. 1968. 140 pp. Gld. 20.—

72. ROMAN JAKOBSON: Child Language, Aphasia and Phonological Universals. 1968. 104 pp. Gld. 12.—

73. CHARLES F. HOCKETT: The State of the Art. 1968. 124 pp. Gld. 18.—

74. A. JUILLAND and HANS-HEINRICH LIEB: "Klasse" und "Klassifikation" in der Sprachwissenschaft. 1968. 75 pp. Gld. 14.—

76. URSULA OOMEN: Automatische Syntaktische Analyse. 1968. 84 pp. Gld. 16.—

77. ALDO D. SCAGLIONE: Ars Grammatica. 1970. 151 pp. Gld. 18.—

106. HENRIK BIRNBAUM: Problems of Typological and Genetic Linguistics Viewed in a Generative Framework. 1971. 132 pp. Gld. 16.—

107. NOAM CHOMSKY: Studies on Semantics in Generative Grammar. 1972. 207 pp. Gld. 24.—

110. MANFRED BIERWISCH: Modern Linguistics. Its Development, Methods and Problems. 1971. 105 pp. Gld. 12.—

113. ERHARD AGRICOLA: Semantische Relationen im Text und im System. 1972. 127 pp. Gld. 26.—

114. ROMAN JAKOBSON: Studies on Child Language and Aphasia. 1971. 132 pp. Gld. 16.—

117. D. L. OLMSTED: Out of the Mouth of Babes. 1971. 260 pp. Gld. 36.—

119. HERMAN PARRET: Language and Discourse. 1971. 292 pp. Gld. 32.—

123. JOHN W. OLLER: Coding Information in Natural Languages. 1971. 120 pp. Gld. 20.—

134. ROMAN JAKOBSON: A Bibliography of His Writings. With a Foreword by C. H. Van Schooneveld. 1971. 60 pp. Gld. 10.—

MOUTON · PUBLISHERS · THE HAGUE